COWBOYS & CONDUCTORS

COWBOYS & CONDUCTORS

Conversations on Horseman-Humanship

Cultivating GREY LEADERSHIP®

DUSTIN DAVIS & PAUL JAN ZDUNEK

atmosphere press

TABLE OF CONTENTS

Conversations...

On Trust & Respect

On the Power of Empowerment

On Discriminating Leadership

On Potential

On Perspective

We lovingly dedicate this book to our wives Aimee and Cindy who empowered us to move our feet and finally put pen to paper. Their encouragement has allowed us to share with you the lessons we have learned about working in a world of grey.

FOREWORD

As an executive producer of some of the world's greatest artists over many decades, including *Chaka Khan, Destiny's Child,* and *Beyoncé*, I have had to be the kind of grey leader Dustin and Paul describe throughout this book.

The world of entertainment is built on grey. On fantasy, where nothing is as it seems. One might even say that's its allure. But in reality, it's a world of extreme highs and bottoming-out lows, exhilarating experiences, and devasting consequences. A world where you're only as good as your last performance. Where your best friends are your safety net, until they're not. It's a world that forces you to have a strong inner core to survive.

But if you can master the art of GREY LEADERSHIP®, you can absolutely thrive!

The entertainment industry is a part of the greater creative economy which also encompasses software designers, architects, biotechnology researchers, and reconstructive surgeons, to name a few. All of these jobs require a work ethic that is full of boundless possibilities while leaving stunting black-and-white decisions behind.

While creative economy workers might more intuitively understand the world of grey, the ideas put forth by Paul and Dustin, along with practical steps you can take within the *Cowboy-Conductor Challenges*, can make a grey leader out of anyone. Whether you want to improve your personal leadership at home, with friends, and in your community, or you want to hone your GREY LEADER-SHIP® skills at work, with your team members, and within your profession, this book will show you how, through the authors' life lessons learned as well as simple challenges you can easily practice and perfect, no matter where you are in the GREY LEADERSHIP® continuum.

Dustin's journey as a real live cowboy, and the approach he uses with all of the horses and livestock under his care, has made him a sought-after expert in natural horsemanship. Throughout his life, he has had many difficult and broken horses to train or re-train due to their owners' ignorance or neglect. Paul's career as an orchestra conductor turned CEO has given him a unique 360° view of life on both sides of the stage lights. His perspective of the human spirit is built from years of transforming countless organizations. Through their intimate and intriguing conversations, Dustin and Paul invite you to sit with them and listen as they discuss what shaped them as the grey leaders they are and how they use this foundational framework to yield transformative results in both their personal and professional lives and in the lives of others.

As a male chest cancer survivor, also known as breast cancer, I have had to rely on these pillars of GREY LEADERSHIP® to enable me to successfully walk through some dire moments that were stressful and draining for me and my family and friends. But I was able to draw on the strength from within, along with the support of my loved ones, to thrive in this new grey paradigm of life.

Don't be fooled by Paul and Dustin's casual tone in this book. Their down-to-earth approach to an incredibly complex topic that plagues every personal and professional leader on this planet is not only easy to understand and implement, it's also both comforting and challenging at the same time. That's what makes *Cowboys & Conductors* so inspirational. You'll want to be a better person and team player not only for yourself, but for your colleagues and loved ones too. And I assure you that every step along the way Dustin and Paul will be cheering you on!

Lastly, at a time where there seems to be more of a focus on the words *them* than *us*, Paul and Dustin encourage all of us to view our collective world through the lens of horseman-humanship, where we are present, supportive, and uplifting to one another. As the wise, Greek storyteller Aesop penned centuries ago, *United we stand, divided we fall.* Simple, yet so profound, and arguably more meaningful today than in any time in our history.

So, pull up a chair, open your mind and enter into the transformational universe of GREY LEADERSHIP®.

~ Mathew Knowles, Ph.D.

Author, professor, lecturer, public speaker, entrepreneur, music executive, artist manager and founder of Music World Entertainment would be the words used to sum up the professional career of Mathew Knowles, Ph.D.

Music World Entertainment is one of the world's leading music and entertainment conglomerates, with record sales exceeding 450 million worldwide, having worked with Chaka Khan, Earth Wind & Fire, The O'Jays, Destiny's Child, and his daughters Solange and Beyoncé, as well as many more.

WHY WE WROTE
THIS BOOK

A grey day provides the best light. ~Leonardo da Vinci

When we first met, on what was a typically warm and sunny day in Southern California, we did not realize the life-changing trajectory a seemingly routine client-consultant business strategy session would set us on.

Picture the scene. An expansive ranch where one hundred horses and fifty cattle peacefully roam. One of us was mounted on a horse donning a cowboy hat while the other dressed in a suit and tie had his feet planted firmly on the ground. A horse-whispering cowboy and an entrepreneurial orchestra conductor turned CEO.

Our professional careers and the journeys leading up to them could not be further apart, yet we immediately realized from the polite introductory conversation that turned into deeply probing and intensely curious questions about each other's approach to life and work that there was a profound connection and bond between us that would last a lifetime.

Our similar perspectives on horses and humans were uncanny. Our questions quickly piled up. We kept interrupting each other out of excitement for the next revelation – the next aha-moment!

Through this intense exchange, we realized that we had a shared focus on leading through *grey*. As it turns out, each of us had already started writing notes for a book on the topic, but had put those notes in a drawer and had not done much with them. That is when we had the brilliant idea to write a book together. We believed that by sharing our experiences and philosophies we could con-nect the dots for others. And so we began meeting weekly and having conversations about horses, people, leader-ship, life, intuitiveness, and  the meaning of the universe. Those conversations, and the aha-moments from them, wound up being the foundation of this book and the essentials of GREY LEADERSHIP®.

This book is about lessons learned throughout our collective lives and careers. It is about the human-horse connection. It is about how one thing can lead to another and to another and so on. It is about possibility, purpose, and passion. It covers our personal and professional journeys and unveils what a cowboy and a conductor turned CEO may have in common.

All of our experiences have shaped each of us into the grey leaders we are today.

GREY LEADERSHIP® is the boundless, non-binary

approach to complex issues using a foundational framework yielding transformational results. It engenders curiosity, creativity, emotional intelligence, and a grounded sense of being. This allows for all of us to take action based on vision, support others to thrive, and design solutions that break through old paradigms.

Leadership is an art. Like painting, sculpting, or playing a musical instrument, it takes intentional practice to perfect. GREY LEADERSHIP® can be learned. It requires the awareness of what it means, the desire to cultivate it, the knowledge of how to attain it, and the ability to use it correctly. Grey Leaders are able to authentically meet people where they are and walk with them to where they need to be. It requires empathy, humility, centeredness, and presence.

The conversations we have included in this book cover the concepts of GREY LEADERSHIP® that we believe are vital for success including *allowing your feet to move freely* and *holding yourself and others in an authentic state of presence.* We discuss these and many more that are critical for changing your personal and professional paradigm.

Our desire is that you find this book to be engaging, informative, and, above all, useful.

While this book can be read in any order, it is organized in three distinct sections and follows a pattern that allows for a progressive understanding from chapter to chapter.

Each chapter is comprised of four components:

Saddling Up acts as an overture, spotlighting the chapter's theme. It contains a thoughtful message to introduce our conversation that follows.

Conversation gives you a front-row view of our real-time conversation about the topic at hand. It is casual, authentic, and strives to be insightful.

Connecting the Dots does just that - it summarizes our conversation and the topic's main points.

Cowboy-Conductor Challenge provides you with our simple, actionable steps to influence and improve your own personal and professional GREY LEADERSHIP® performance.

Now you know what you get when you mix a horse-whispering cowboy with an entrepreneurial conductor - a book on cultivating GREY LEADERSHIP®.

Enjoy!

SETTING THE STAGE

The vast majority of us naturally give into our black-and-white binary approach to thinking and decision-making. It makes us feel safe and secure. Grey is our enemy. Yet operating in grey is the secret strategy used by highly successful leaders.

To set the stage for our reflections on GREY LEADERSHIP®, conductor, composer, cellist, and poet, David Lockington, offers his perspective of delighting in the grey.

Grey

I am attuned to grey
When I walk in grey I breathe deeper
The lack of vividness leaves room for me to feel
my thoughts
I become vivid
Grey wraps me in my childhood
Its denseness is my comforter
keeping me warm and safe
What is misty ahead
parts and becomes clear in my mind
or I can drift if I choose
in ambiguity
Sounds are punctuated by a different
silence
more like a sound-proofed padded cell
The birds sound cheerful
despite being straight-jacketed in grey
And this is my ideal
to be happy in grey
To be happy in a small, padded room
needing little
creating vivid from within
happy with memory and
now

~ David Lockington

We encourage you to Be the GREY™

ON BEING A COWBOY

Saddling Up

Unless you have had the privilege of living on wide-open land or expansive pastures, you probably have never met a real-live cowboy. Most of us have met teachers, accountants, law enforcement personnel, and mail carriers, but certainly not a professional, life-long cowboy like Dustin Davis. How do you become a cowboy? What does it take? What's the reality behind Hollywood's Wild West version of a life like this? Let's find out!

Conversation

Paul:

For those of us who are laypeople, what does identifying as a cowboy mean to you?

Dustin:

A cowboy to me is a man who lives for his values, his honor, his loyalty, his morals, his courage, and he stands for something. Also, being a man who treats his live-stock like family. As  far back as I can recall I've always wanted to be a cowboy. Where I grew up, we had neighbors that managed a great big ranch. So I would spend my summers with them. We rode and roped calves and did all kinds of ranch kid stuff. When I was just a little guy, my folks got me a horse, and I'd get up every morning and I'd take off to the barn with my dog and my goat, get my horse, and head out across the pasture. My dog, my goat, and my horse would go with me everywhere. Mom said all she'd have to do was look out the window when she needed me for when she saw one of those animals, she knew where I was because they were always with me.

I grew up around a lot of that cowboy lifestyle. When

4

I was a little bit older, my dad was an auctioneer. I'd go with him and ride horses through the sale ring for the public. This was no small feat since adults couldn't ride some of these horses. I'd ride these horses through the sale ring because if a young person was riding them they were worth more money, but I was thankful my dad was the auctioneer and had my back because a lot of the horses I shouldn't have been riding. They were young horses that didn't know very much, but for some reason I was able to ride them. It was apparent from a young age I was handy and had a deeper connection with the horse than most. Through junior high and high school I participated in 4H. There I learned to manage things and to be successful with my market hogs and roping. That helped me to pave the way into other endeavors in life by setting the foundation of what it was to help people, public speaking, to be an open person, to be a gracious winner and loser, to tend to your livestock and manage it well so they marketed well to the judges and the public. There I earned many accolades and caught the attention of local businesses that purchased my animals year after year. I graduated high school early and had caught the eye of the Colorado State University livestock judging coach. I had the opportunity to decide between going to CSU or auctioneer college. Growing up around the auction business and having sold my first sale before I was a teenager and finding a passion for it wound up being why I chose to follow in my father's and grandfather's footsteps and head to auctioneer college. I then found myself in the auction block at the sales, instead of riding the horses through the sales, and gaining more knowledge of how the auction business worked. Shortly after school, an opportunity presented itself to work on a very notable ranch in Colorado that was thirty-eight thousand acres. We ran a lot of cows and built a lot of fence. But everybody always told me there's no money in being a cowboy. And, there's not. You gotta do it because you love it. You're not going to get rich. It's not a lavish job. Most of the time, you get provided housing, you get decent pay, you get free beef, and you get a company truck. And that's a good outfit. You also get a string of horses at a good outfit. Other places you gotta take your own horses. You gotta do it for the romance of it and that sounds cliché, but there's nothing better than seeing a horse or a calf born and being there for the first moments of life and knowing that you're keeping things going in this world. Just seeing something so pure, that's been here for so long, and being able to develop those relationships. There's so much to learn from it.

But everybody kept telling me you can't make any money riding horses or being a cowboy. So I tried some other stuff. And, yeah, it worked out all right and I learned a lot of things. But I kept finding my way back around to the horses. Then I had a major horse accident just after I turned twenty-one that took me away from horses for a couple of years. Within that time I moved to Oklahoma and tried to start life over again. But I found my way back to horses having to relearn a lot of things and overcome major fears when I found myself back on a horse. I had an empathy and a new understanding for the horse and the role horses would play in my life. While in Oklahoma, I ran across an old family friend who was deep into the horse business. I found a job working for them hauling horses to the airport for export all over the world. Within a few short months, I opened the doors to my equine transport that, within two years' time and with the help of a great mentor on the other side of the business, became one of the largest importers and exporters of horses in the world. It was an incredible life experience that literally put thousands of horses through my hands and gave me the opportunity to meet and be around some of the most respected horsemen in the world.

Then, due to the economy, the bottom fell out of exporting and we closed the doors to the transport business. It wasn't long after I found my way back to my roots, day-working on ranches. It was around this time that I got introduced to Tom Dorrance and Ray Hunt's style of horsemanship and the Californio Bridle Horse - this was all new to me. This style of horsemanship and partnership with the horse was unlike anything I'd ever seen before. I didn't know what those guys had going on with their horses, but I wanted it with the horses I rode. Little did I know I would meet my wife Aimee and move to California where I would become immersed in this style of horsemanship. Everything fell into place immediately in California. There was no shortage of horses that needed my help allowing me to learn from each new horse and work at this new style of horsemanship. With my wife being in the horse industry as well, we have adapted this style of horsemanship to the ninety plus horses we own, and we both have had major success with it. Like the great horseman Ray Hunt said, "I haven't found a horse this style won't fit." This started me on a lifelong journey and quest for knowledge to better myself for the horse.

Paul:
What was the driver that kept you coming back to horses?

Dustin:

I don't know that I can put a finger on exactly what kept driving me back to horses.

There's always been something that keeps bringing me back here. I guess, to me, there's a calmness and a peacefulness. I crave the partnership with the horses. The horse being a mirrored image of you has kept me striving to be better personally and professionally. To me the horse is so pure. There is no ego. The horse truly wants to please the human despite what most think. They, like the human, learn from what they live; therefore, I find that most horses are the way they are from what they have lived and experienced, a lot like a human.

Paul:

Do you think the calmness and peacefulness centers you?

Dustin:

Yes, when I'm with the horse, time to me is irrelevant. When I'm around horses everything around me is just white noise. I'm living in the moment with the horse and willing to take the time it takes to help the horse.

And even when I was a little fart, I always wanted to be around horses, and I've always wanted to since. I think a lot of people say, "You're born with that kind of stuff." I don't know if that's true or not. And there's a lot of family history that goes back to horses and horsemanship for me. Something always draws me back to them. And whenever I haven't had them in my life, that's when I was probably the most lost, if you will, or I just didn't feel like things were the right way. And then I found my way back to them and here I am.

But being a cowboy, yeah, I guess it just tickles me to death that people pay me to ride their horses every day. I get to do something that I absolutely love. I mean, I never worked a day in my life because I do what I love. I work way more hours and make way less money than most people in this world, but I feel like I've never worked a day in my life. So when you live a life in that aspect, it doesn't get much better as far as I'm concerned.

Paul:
That is the sweet spot in life: doing what you are the best in the world at and what you are the most passionate about. I often mentor young professionals or graduating students about this very point. Additionally, if you can match what you completely excel in and absolutely love to do with something that provides you with a living wage, then that, my friend, is the trifecta!

Connecting the Dots

How many people do we know who are unhappy at their job? Those who cannot wait for 5:00 PM to roll around so they can get back to their real life? Most likely everyone we know. It is rare to meet someone who loves their job and excels at it. However, despite the countless career counselors employed in our high schools and colleges, many of us wander blindly into our careers. It may be because of a course we recently enrolled in, a friend's work we admire or perhaps it is in our family history. But, most of us do not know who or what we want to be until our last year of college or maybe not at all. As long as we are making a decent living, providing for ourselves and for our family, that is enough.

What if we, instead, took inventory of what we are passionate about, match that with what we excel at, and topped it off with what would bring us financial gain? That really would be the trifecta. We would be awesome at our job, we would absolutely love doing it day in and day out, *and* we would get paid for it!

Although Dustin had a few detours, some of which were tragic, he always came back to being a cowboy. His passion for horses, and all they embody, drove him back every time. His approach to horse training set him above the professional herd. He had opportunities to work in other jobs and industries, but he decided to follow his instinct, his natural skills, and choose the life of a cowboy. While the economics of this career are not the most lucrative, the love of his job supersedes this obstacle. Yes, money makes the world go around, but having the feeling that you have never worked a day in your life because you are so satisfied with your job is priceless!

Cowboy-Conductor Challenge

One of the most important drivers of a fulfilling career must include an absolute love of what you do. You can be the best in the world at something, but if you hate doing it, you will always be miserable, no matter how much money you are making.

First, make a list of all the things you love to do and are over-the-moon passionate about. This list might include something as simple as exercising or as complex as bringing all of humanity together in peace and harmony.

Then, make a list of everything you believe you are the best in the world at, where you are in the top tenth percentile of your peers. This list might include something as simple as easily connecting with people you have never met before or as complex as being able to compose and conduct Oscar-worthy movie scores.

Next, compare the two lists to see if there is a job that will pay you to combine your passions and skills. Look for the subtle connections. For instance, you might love tasting as many exotic foods as you can get your hands on, and you also might completely excel at writing. Well then, you may want to look at being a food critic for a global leisure company.

Does your list of skills feel too short? Maybe your gift or talent does not feel like one to you. Perhaps you can ask your family or friends to list what they think you are best in the world at. Sometimes what we excel at feels normal to us, not extraordinary.

Make your lists. Connect your dots. Discover your future.

ON HORSEMANSHIP

Saddling Up

Even if you had not grown up on a farm or in the country, many of us have had a chance to ride a horse. Perhaps that might have been when you were little and got to ride the miniature ponies at the county fair or when you went horseback riding with friends at a local stable or on the beach in Mexico. But few actually own a horse, much less know how to raise it, train it, and care for it. Horsemanship in its simplest form is the art of riding, handling, and training horses, but it goes beyond that. It is all about the approach. It is the *how*, not the *what* that truly matters.

Conversation

Paul:

What is your definition of horsemanship?

Dustin:

It's funny that you ask that because I was thinking pretty hard on that the other day trying to come up with a definition of it.

Horsemanship is a term that is thrown around a lot nowadays. To me, to be called a horseman is a pretty high honor. I'll spend my life working on becoming one. The people in my world that I call horseman, well, it takes a large stick to even play in their park. I'm talking about Ray Hunt, Tom Dorrance, Buck Brannaman, Lee Smith, George Morris, Gwynn Turnbull Weaver, Dave Weaver, and Buster McLaury to name a few. With folks like that as horsemen, the bar is set extremely high. But to me, as far as horsemanship first and foremost, horses have to be number one in your world. Number one in that you want to take care of them, and the fact that they're your responsibility and their needs come before your own. To me, it's how you take care of them, the way you present things to them, the way you handle situations with them, and the way you get along with them that is critical.

I hear people say all the time that they are horsemen, but I watch them and I'm lucky if I can sit there for five minutes because they're just jerking the horses' mouths or kicking them in the belly with their spurs left and right for no reason. All they're doing is troubling the horse. They are making them scared and not trying to see things from the horse's perspective. And that's not being a horseman or good horsemanship. If they knew something better, they'd do something better, but they don't. So if that's how they act, I say, "Don't call yourself a horseman 'cause you damn sure ain't. Because if you were, you wouldn't be doing that stuff." So to me, it's a lot about how you treat the horse, the respect you have for the horse, and the nobility that the horse has in your world.

There's a lot of people that are all about their horsemanship, and they may put on a facade when they're in front of people, but when they get around the corner, it changes. But it can't; you've gotta hold yourself to the same standard out of the public eye too. Every day, day in day and day out, it doesn't matter who's watching you. It's got to come from within you. That's what it's about.

You can't cut a corner and cheat a horse to try and get something sooner. You have to take the right path and give the horse what the horse deserves. And that's respect for the horse. But most people cheat and do something else when they know people aren't watching. Real horsemanship isn't about that.

Paul:
That works in life as well, doesn't it? Slow and steady and authenticity win the race; and, cheating and stealing and faking your way to the top only creates a faster and deeper fall.

Dustin:
I like that a lot. I hadn't heard that one, but yeah, it's the same thing.

Connecting the Dots

It is much easier to bully someone into doing something than to meet them where they are and gently convince them. It also takes less time. So why not manage this way if it is so much more *efficient* in the moment? Because it is not more *effective*. Bullying may get you your way, but it does not create trusting relationships which are the foundation of our entire human infrastructure. Because humans are generally conflict-averse, we tend to use power instead of persuasion in our workplace, in our home, and definitely with those with whom we have little to no relationship. What does it take to change this dynamic? It takes empathy. It takes understanding. It takes love.

Horsemanship, as Dustin describes it, is making that horse your number one priority, your absolute focus which then drives how you approach them, how you respond to them, and how you develop your partnership with them. While it might be easy to do this at home with your young child, your own flesh and blood, it might not be as easy when working with a colleague who is a complete asshole. But what if you tried a horsemanship approach with that co-worker? It would probably be shocking for both of you!

This approach needs to be authentic. How many of you have been through company retreats that start off with an icebreaker designed to get you to open up to each other in ways that are personal and can feel really uncomfortable? Most of us hate this exercise. But what if we drew on our empathy, and realized that everyone else is feeling the exact same way? Then maybe this collective embarrassment could turn into an authentic sharing of something that is not only personal, but also meaningful to our peers. This one moment could then be the nucleus for lifelong, trusting relationships with our fellow retreaters because we decided to be authentically vulnerable which then made everyone else after us who answered the icebreaker question much more relaxed.

Cowboy-Conductor Challenge

Identify someone in your life who has been difficult to get along with or to connect to. While it might be easy to think of all the things that make them challenging, try looking beyond the obvious to find one tiny, little thing that you both agree on, enjoy, or have in common. Maybe this is a type of coffee you both like, a favorite book you both thought was engaging, or maybe it is a common annoyance at work that drives you both mad. Start there. Comment on it the next time you see that person. Watch for signs of relaxation in the other person's tone, pitch, or body language. Then build on it.

It may seem counterintuitive, but we assure you it will throw them off guard. That is your moment to walk further into their life. It is the moment you lay that first brick of trust that can eventually turn into a fortified foundation in the future.

How does it feel to connect with that person in this way? Did it go the way you hoped? Most likely the first try will be uncomfortable, but try to engage again, and then again. Continue to adjust your approach.

If horsemanship is making the horse, or in this case the person, the most important focus in your life, imagine how they will react when you connect with them in this authentic way?

Try it. The worst that can happen is that you showed a kindness to someone who did not return it. No one died.

ON BEING A CONDUCTOR

Saddling Up

Unless you are in the entertainment business, chances are you have never had the opportunity to have an up-close and personal conversation with a conductor like Paul Jan Zdunek. The music kind, not the locomotive kind. Most of us probably have the iconic Bugs Bunny in our head when we think about a conductor. We imagine a tall person with white, untamed hair dressed in a tuxedo dramatically waving a long stick while standing on a box in front of a huge assembly of musicians. But there is so much more to it than that. What does that path to the podium look like? Where would you even begin?

Conversation

Dustin:
How did you get into conducting and what took you there?

Paul:
Well, I grew up in Baltimore, and was running the streets in the city as a kid.

We did a lot of stuff that you shouldn't be doing. Some legal, some illegal, mostly just dumb kid stuff. But when I was about twelve years old, a new choir director in town started a boy choir at my church. He was young and passionate about all that music and life had to offer. He was committed to cultivating our natural potential. So this ragtag group I was with went from shoplifting on a Friday night for fun to singing Mozart, Beethoven, and Palestrina – so many wonderful composers. As a boy soprano, I was hitting all of these high notes and it was nothing short of mind-blowing! When the choir director saw that I had musical talent, he got me into piano lessons with his teacher. He would also take us on outings to downtown which was only two or three miles away. I mean, I could have walked there and I didn't even know it existed. He

showed us the opera and the symphony and all of the theaters and museums. I never realized that there was this whole world virtually at my doorstep. I was mesmerized, so I kept getting deeper into music. My mother encouraged all of it. But before I started piano lessons, I had to overcome the hurdle of getting a piano that I could practice on at home.

Luckily, at my middle school there was an old, tattered upright piano in the backstage corner of their theater. One day I just asked the principal, "Are you ever going to use this piano because it seems to be all covered up and dusty," and she said, "Probably not." So I said, "Well, do you mind if I take it?" And like a dream, she said, "Sure, have at it."

So I rolled this piano, this upright piano, on its tiny one-inch wooden castor wheels down the streets of my Baltimore City neighborhood with a friend of mine and somehow got it into my basement. Everything seemed to make sense in the moment, but as I look back, I think, "What the hell was I doing?" But, anyway, I polished it up and started taking piano lessons.

Within a couple of years of formal music training, a community college catalog arrived in the mail. As I was flipping through it, looking through the music section, I came across a conducting course. Wow! Conducting! I immediately knew I wanted to do that, yet too naïve to fully appreciate what I was getting myself into.

Let me back up a moment. What really got me started as far as my interest in conducting was a moment during a July 4th concert in Baltimore at the Inner Harbor. The entire Baltimore Symphony Orchestra was there and they were doing this big patriotic concert and the conductor was completely throwing himself into the music. This performance had a huge string sound, exciting brass, and percussion riffs, as well as exploding cannons and fireworks! Then, all of a sudden, I felt this overpowering energy come from the back of the orchestra, through the conductor, and into the audience and I was blown away. I had never ever felt anything like that before. It was physical, emotional, and spiritual all at the same time. It was as though the universe was sending me a message. At that very powerful, transformative moment, I knew that's what I wanted to do. It was awesome to see and feel that vibrancy. That is what got me thinking about conducting as a life path.

Just as importantly, I pursued conducting because I wanted to be that boy choir director, that mentor who pulled me off the street. That's literally what he did for me. I knew immediately that I wanted to do that for somebody else. That was the deep-rooted impetus of my future conducting career - to give back what I had received.

So when this community college catalog came along, I thought how great is it that you can just take a course and then you're a conductor. That's awesome. So, again, I didn't know shit. I was two years into piano lessons and I hardly knew anything, but I called the teacher, and he asked if I'd had any music theory lessons. And I said, "Yes, I've had some theory lessons from my piano teacher." He said, "Great, sign up for the class." I wound up in this course with these college kids when I was a mere sixteen years old and managed through it, and learned a lot. The teacher actually turned out to be the second clarinetist and associate conductor of the Baltimore Symphony Orchestra, so I got really excellent training from the start. I just wandered into it.

On another note, so to speak, when I was younger, I was very entrepreneurial and always trying to make money. I had a job at a dry cleaners. I'd go after school every day and on the weekend. I also worked as a sales operator at Olan Mills Portrait Studio, calling families during their dinner and tv-watching hours to sell them a package they didn't really need. I found out that I was good

at convincing people. I actually still have my certificate from when I was celebrated as the top salesperson of the week. As a kid! I also made fried dough in my mother's kitchen once and completely ruined it, but I did make twelve dollars selling it to the neighbors! That was a lot of money for a day's work at the age of eleven. I was always trying to make money. However, my mother didn't really encourage that because I was destroying her house. Looking back, I can see why she was frustrated.

Fast-forward, after ten years of conducting professionally, that entrepreneurial kid came back out again and I was so distracted by it that I had to explore it, and that's when I wound up hanging up my baton and jumping into business which was my first true love. I landed a job for a company that produced architectural stone. The visionary owner of the company hired me. I'll never forget my interview. He said, "I need someone to deal with the egos of all of these architects around the country. You're a conductor. You've managed musicians' egos all of these years. You're the perfect fit!" So, that's what I did. And within several months, I was asked to serve on the Senior Executive Council for Vision & Long-range Planning.

Dustin:
Well, that's life's path. It's part of the journey that got you to where you're at.

Everyone's got a different journey of how they got to where they are, and to me it's always fascinating to hear about it. Because you don't know where life is going to take you. It's just part of life's ride.

Paul:
I think most of us wander around and, hopefully, we wander through the right doors. I used to feel like there was or needed to be a straight path from birth to death with my career. Well, I'm finding that some of the more interesting and successful people have wandered around and just happened to wander through the right doors at the right times.

Dustin:
Kind of like that diagram I showed you the other day. Everybody's got that straight trajectory in mind, but that is not what's going to happen. I guarantee you.

Paul:
Exactly.

Dustin:
So before we move on to your business side of it, what did being a conductor mean to you? What did it mean to you when you were doing it?

Paul:

Well, interestingly enough, my undergraduate was in composition, I was composing music. However, I didn't want to pursue being a professional composer. I wasn't looking to sell my work or be a famous composer. What I really wanted to do was to understand the score from the other side. I wanted to know what it feels like to create something and then turn that over to someone else to perform it, interpret it. You know, conducting, just like performing, is interpreting or reimagining what someone else has created. It's finding the underlying message, the underlying theme of what that person was trying to say with his or her work of music. And so being a composer and writing music, I was thinking, "Oh, this interpretation is really obvious. I'm making very specific notes on how this should sound and how this should be played." But...I remember turning my composition over the first time to musicians to perform it and I thought, "What the hell is this?!" That's not how I thought it was going to go. And not even the notes, but it was the interpretation that threw me. And, so, I thought we have the compositions of people who have been dead for two to three hundred years. They don't have the opportunity to say, "Hey, that's not how it goes, mate!"

It taught me something I have carried with me ever since. When somebody tells me they have it all figured out - like this is the absolute right way to perform Beethoven - I am usually suspicious. My experience has taught me that there is no absolute right way because it is somebody else's interpretation of what you said or did or wrote. That was a life-changing moment for me.

So as a conductor, to answer your original question,

it's not only trying to be true to what that composer wanted, but also to add my own personal style to it, my own personal voice to it, which is what recreating art is all about. You take something that's basically formed, and you maneuver it a little bit, or a lot-a-bit, and that's where you get artistry. Technique is the tool that allows you to recreate, but artistry is what actually moves people emotionally, intellectually, and even physically. And so being able to touch that audience member and give that audience member an "aha-moment" like I had when I was a kid – that's what drove me as a conductor and still drives me today as a business strategist.

Dustin:

That drives me too! In a lot of ways I'm emulating what past masters and mentors have done for years, but I try and put my own little touches in here and there with these horses. For me, there's those "aha-moments" I have, too, when working with a horse. But then I also love to set it up in a way where the owner, when they're taking their lesson with their horse, has that "aha-moment." And it's probably the biggest thrill for me to see them actually feel that horse do something for them or they get something correct. I know what you mean, it's like, "Ah, there it is!" And you can just see it. You can feel it with every ounce of them and the horse. Everything just got right and I'm sure it's the same thing with the music as you said. It's that "aha" when the musicians or audience members hear what you've done, and it's as though they say, "You got it! That's right! That's what we were looking for!"

25

Paul:

And you know, this "aha-moment" is actually how I work on the business side too.

When I facilitate meetings or board retreats, I want them to get to that "aha-moment" and have it surprise the hell out of them, and I guide them in such a way that they come to it themselves. It's kind of what you were talking about before where you work with the horse and all of a sudden you've got that moment when the skies open up and you didn't see it coming. It just happened. That "aha-moment." That is what artistry is all about and what working with human beings is all about. Always trying to get them to that incredibly surprising and powerful place they didn't know was possible.

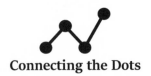

Connecting the Dots

When we think about what we want to be when we grow up, most of us tackle this question midway through our college degree. Some of us have figured it out by the time we are graduating high school. But if you want to be a musician, that question has to be answered sooner rather than later. Most professional musicians start their training before the age of seven, some even as early as three. In Paul's case, he started at the late age of twelve. So while there was some catching up to do, he had a driving motive for accomplishing this goal. He had a mentor, someone who showed him the possibilities that existed out there in the world which then led him to his own "aha-moment." Paul was so grateful for this that he decided to become a conductor so he could have the platform or podium, so to speak, to lift up others the way he had been.

The challenge was that he also had other passions that predated his involvement with music but were not supported, nor even recognized: inventing a new way of doing things, producing products people wanted, making money - in other words, entrepreneurship. Interestingly enough, though, being a conductor and being an entrepreneur are not that different. The connection of being a conductor and being an entrepreneur is that breakthrough moment that gives you and others involved in your work that "aha-moment." That is *the* game-changer. However, to get to that moment requires you to walk through many doors, explore many options, and never let failure stop you from achieving your dreams. Additionally, like Paul, you have to believe that anything is possible, even becoming a full-fledged conductor by only taking one college course.

Simple. Right? No. But believing it is more than halfway to accomplishing it.

Cowboy-Conductor Challenge

Think about a time when you thought a personal or career choice should have gone your way, but instead it wound up being dead-on-arrival. Perhaps it was that love of your life or that perfect job. Examine the micro-steps that led to its demise. Then reflect on whether those steps aided or hindered the ultimate outcome.

Did you feel that while you really wanted that "perfect" job, the connection to the company and its team was lackluster during the interview process? Do not ignore those signs. They pop up for a reason. The more you can identify those warning signals during the process, the better for you and everyone else in the long run.

As the saying goes, when one door shuts, another door opens. But often we are so distraught about the first door slamming in our face that we do not see that the other door has, ever so slightly, cracked open. Perhaps we have not even noticed the other door at all.

Take inventory of all of your negative experiences and compare them to all of your positive experiences and see if there is a life blueprint to guide your future choices. Most likely, there is. Ask yourself, "Why did that happen or why did it not happen?" This examination will allow you to understand that when something does not go as expected, there is probably a reason for it. See if you can find a pattern, no matter how subtle. Did you really want it? Did you give it your best? Did you have an uneasy feeling from the start? The answer will present itself. So do not stress. Do not panic or make hasty decisions.

Realize that the universe is saying to you, "Another door has opened. Walk through it."

ON HUMANSHIP

Saddling Up

The state of any relationship affects everything around it. If you are in love with someone, your view of the world is joyful and you tend to be more present. If you are angry with someone, you begin to find disagreements with others and tend to disconnect. How you interact with others based on your inner feelings shapes the culture within your home, your workplace, and your community. These relationships, these humanships, are what determine our successes and our failures as individuals and as a society.

Conversation

Dustin:
Although it's a more recent term, and might not even be in the dictionary, what does humanship mean to you?

Paul:
I think, at its foundation, humanship is the essence of *who* we are, not *what* we are. It's not based on how we usually identify ourselves outwardly such as our race, ethnicity, nationality, religious or political beliefs, job title, role or function. It's based on what all humans share, such as the ability to love, to have empathy, to be afraid, and to experience a full range of emotions from anger to joy and everything in between. It's the ability to overcome obstacles, to strategically think our way through a challenge, and to be creative as well as analytical. Humanship is what connects all of us no matter what we are or where we are.

If you really think about your fellow human in this very basic way, then how can we allow discrimination, hate, violence, disdain, judgment, or jealousy to come between us? Why don't we focus on what unites us, not what tears us apart?

Humanship is looking past each other's power-position, wealth, and social status to focus on the fact that we all universally seem to agree on similar pursuits of life, freedom, and happiness. We share the pursuit of creating, celebrating, living, and protecting life. We embrace the pursuit of boundless freedom that allows us to think, say, and do whatever we want without infringing on others. We pursue blissful happiness as we do all we can to avoid physical, mental, and emotional negativities that cause us pain and suffering.

Although viewing the world in this way is often criticized as Pollyannaish, idealistic, and sometimes just plain wacky, who wouldn't want to approach life this way, to live in a world like this!

Dustin:
Exactly. Count me in!

Paul:
To me, humanship is very much how you described horsemanship. First and foremost, the love and care for your fellow human has to be paramount to how you relate to the human herd. Drawing a parallel to your description, humanship is born out in how we care for each other, look after each other, present things to each other, and handle situations, good and bad, with each other.

As a conductor and as a CEO, for me humanship is also helping people see the possibilities, to help them achieve what they think is far beyond their capabilities. Humanship, like horsemanship, is the approach one takes to get people there. It's not using your position, power, or pressure. It's using trust, legislative leadership, and empathy. As a conductor or CEO, one might assume that since you are ultimately responsible for the entire musical or management team, as well as the entire institution, that you must lead with both a carrot and a stick. Reward and punishment. Actually, I've witnessed many conductors and CEOs who manage with the stick alone. Those are usually the most unsuccessful ones. However, what if we took a humanship approach and didn't think about leading with a carrot or a stick, but authentically met people where they are, took their hand, and walked together through the challenge? Wouldn't life be so much different than it is today?

Dustin:

I can't even imagine what that would look like.

Paul:

This may sound silly, but I also believe there are a finite number of char-acters, or perhaps caricatures, in the world. For in-stance, in every orchestra, work-place, or commu-nity, there is al-ways that cur-mudgeon, that optimist, that schemer, or that complete bore. Haven't you ever arrived at a party and immediately tried finding the kind of person that you most identify with? If you're a pessimist, you make a beeline to your pessimistic friends, bypassing all the other happy-go-luckys in the room, right?

My point in this is to say, we are all in this together.

Dustin:

How does this translate in the greater world of politics, religion, or global leadership?

Paul:
Humanship is about us, not us and them. There is no them in humanship. If we focus on each other, our inner connections, no matter what our outward persona is, I guarantee we will treat each other better, look out for each other better, and lift each other up better in every aspect of life.

Dustin:
That's powerful.

Connecting the Dots

In 1954, Leon Festinger proposed the Social Comparison Theory which centers on the belief that there is a drive within individuals to gain accurate self-evaluations by comparing themselves to others in order to define their own self. Little did Festinger know how much social media would compound this. He went on to hypothesize that we tend to compare ourselves to those with whom we most identify. But the question is, how are we measuring who is like us? Is it status? Is it the color of our skin? Is it the zip code we live in? Or is it something more inward, such as our collective need for belonging?

Humanship is about finding those inward connections to each other. It is how we approach one another, work with one another, and live with one another. Our outward self is a façade to what is beneath. We may look very different from others around the world, but our need for safety is the same. Sadly enough, Festinger also hypothesized that the more our appearance differs from one another, the less we compare ourselves. In other words, a young Spanish male might think he has no connection to an older Norwegian female. If we subscribe to this belief, then it is unlikely we will try to understand what connects us, what unites us. We must fight against Festinger's hypothesis and look beyond our outward façades to find those foundational qualities that we all share as human beings.

The United States Constitution begins with, "We, the People...in Order to form a more perfect Union...." Think about those simple words and what a powerful message they send. We. People. Union. It then goes on to list what we all desire - *all* of us. Justice. Tranquility. Liberty. Let us view our fellow humans through this lens of connectivity and similarities. Can you imagine what we could accomplish if we all saw each other as *us* instead of *them*? The possibilities would be infinite.

Cowboy-Conductor Challenge

The next time you find yourself among people you do not know well, instead of making a beeline for those with whom you easily identify, find someone that you think is the complete opposite of you. Perhaps they are different racially, ethnically, nationally, or they are in a different industry, position, or social class from you.

Push yourself to start a conversation with them. You can warm up with what we all have in common: the weather and traffic. Then, without being creepy, ask about their inner self. What drives them? What are they passionate about? What would they do if a genie gave them three wishes?

What kind of common humanship did you find? How did that feel? Surprising? Comforting?

What you are most likely going to find out is that the foundation of their answers is more similar to yours than not. That is where you will find connectivity and togetherness. The more you view people through this empathetic lens, the less useful the word "them" will be in your vocabulary.

This is an exercise that can and should be repeated. Remember, practice makes perfect.

ON TRUST & RESPECT

Saddling Up

For whatever reason, we tend to be very judgmental of each other, perhaps because it makes us feel superior, which feeds our egos. Even though many of us would not outwardly admit that we do this, it happens all the time. We are always judging, always assessing, and then coming to conclusions that may or may not be valid. How you present yourself to others then, through how you dress, how you speak, and how you pose, becomes the basis for how you are judged by others which often impacts whether they will respect and trust you.

Conversation

Paul:

While many believe respect is incredibly important, the foundation of any relationship must begin with trust. Is there a respect or a trust that horses respond to? You once told me that you and your wife Aimee can walk up to a horse and get a different response than others. There must be some kind of relationship in place for that to be able to happen. Is it trust, respect, or is it something else?

Dustin:

It's trust and respect, the same as it would be in a herd dynamic because there is a hierarchy in the herd. For example, the lead horse calls the shots in the herd. The herd respects that horse knowing that if trouble arises they know they can move with that horse to a safer place. When I build a partnership with the horse, I become the lead horse. Through the work I do, I try to help that horse overcome any obstacle and gain confidence in themselves and trust in me. As a result, the horse learns that it can look to me in a time of trouble and I will keep it safe instead of the horse's natural reaction to run from trouble. Through the partnership I've built, they look to me for a way out of trouble.

Paul:

Does a horse assess the human then? The first time you work with a horse, like I work with an orchestra, does that horse assess you that way immediately?

Dustin:

They do assess you, but in a way different from the human. It's not as if they see you and say this guy looks the part, he's going to be a lead horse. It's more as you begin to work with the horse they are assessing you in ways such as do they move my feet or do I move their feet. And to the horse it can go either way. It doesn't matter to them; they just need to know where they stand. And to a horse, which is true with a human, a lot of things depend on your presentation.

It would be like me saying "Paul, I'm going to teach you how to swing a rope." The success of it will be dependent on the presentation. If I just gave you a rope and said this is how you swing it and just went through the motions and presented it in a way you didn't understand, you would be less likely to want to continue. But if we dinked around and I broke it into smaller bites of information and I taught you to rock the loop and roll your arm and be successful with one swing and stop, we would then have a foundation built where you could swing it over your head and it was encouraging. You would then begin to respect and trust me that I could help you through whatever may arise. So with a horse, I start out with simple movements so that the horse understands the presentation and the expectations I have for the relationship.

Paul:

Yes, I can see how those two teaching styles would produce opposite results.

Let's go back to instincts when you and a horse first meet. There is research that states when humans meet for the first time, there are two things they assess immediately upon seeing each other: can I trust you and do I respect you?

Amy Cuddy, a professor at the Harvard Business School who has been studying the science of first impressions for years, says this is born out of our caveman times. So when out hunting, you earn my respect by actually killing something that day. But if we don't kill anything, can I trust you won't eat me while I'm sleeping that night?

Is that the same with horses? Perhaps they react to your aura or your emotional radiation that allows them to trust or respect you. Is there anything to that?

Dustin:

Yes, there is. And the biggest difference is, as far as emotional stuff, horses don't have the frontal lobe like the human to have the emotional side of things. There's been a lot written on that. Dr. Stephen Peters & Martin Black wrote a phenomenal book titled *Evidence-Based Horsemanship* and produced a DVD titled *Exploring Evidence-Based Horsemanship.* That's probably the one thing if people could understand, to be an incredible horseman, you have to put all emotion aside because emotions just don't work when it comes to horses.

But, with that being said, when I'm working with a horse, I read body language right off the bat. How does that horse present himself? Is he in a relaxed state? Where is he carrying his head? Is he up and he's blowin'? Is he bouncing around?

To me, I read what the body language is telling me about that horse and how he's moving around and what he's doing. Is he slinging his head and kicking out at you as he goes by in disrespect? Or has he got a presence about him as he's moving around that he's very sure of himself so he's obviously a lead-type horse? Or is he a horse that is very pushy in his presence and how he does things? Over time, you learn those things.

It's interesting that you say that about assessing people. Because when I meet people for the first time, their posture is always the first thing I notice about them. I don't know why but I've done this my whole life. And I don't know if it's because I've been harped on about my posture and standing up straight my whole life, but it's always been something that spoke to me about people right off the bat.

Paul:
Given what you said earlier about subtle signals, is it also true for horses, that they've got a posture and posturing that feed into the herd dynamic?

Dustin:
Oh yeah, totally.

Paul:
So you've seen it; you've learned it from both horses and humans.

Dustin:
I've learned it. I've lived it. That's part of it.

The trust that you talk about is interesting. I think about when I meet people for the first time. There's people you'll meet and after a short conversation, you realize they are just skimming the surface of the pond of life. And others that you talk with and there's a depth to the conversation. For example, the ones with no depth, it's just kind of irrelevant conversation, "how's your day," "how's the weather." It doesn't go much further than that.

But then there's other people, like when we first met. Through our conversation about business and horses and the similarities, the meaning of the conversation got deeper into that pond of life leading to a mutual trust and respect and an excitement to write a book together even though we came from much different backgrounds.

Paul:
I love that *pond of life* reference.

Dustin:
I've got some doozies. Aimee always asks, "Where did that come from? I've been with you for years and I've never heard some of these." So there you go.

Paul:
That's awesome! But what you said earlier is true. There is something to body language and facial expressions. Those micro-expressions in your body and face that signal whether you're lying or not. I mean small subtle stuff, not the obvious sweating or nervousness. Actually, there is a large scientific body of information on these subtle expressions. It reminds me of when you once told me about the subtly of a horse pinning its ear back. It's something that people might not pick up on. It's similar to if I slightly raise my eyebrow at the Tuba player all the way in the back of the stage for a dramatic effect.

Fascinating!

Connecting the Dots

We are always telling others about who we are even when we are not saying anything. Our style of clothing, the gaze of our eyes, the way we sit in a chair, and which place we choose at a dining or conference room table all play into what others think about us and how they feel toward us. How we present ourselves matters. If you show up in wrinkled clothes, some may conclude you are sloppy. If you are always looking around the room when in conversation, people may think you do not value them. If you often use *me* and *my* instead of *us* and *our*, you might have everyone believing you are shallow or not a team player. It does not take much for others to condemn you. And if you combine all three of these examples, you may be doomed within minutes of making a poor first impression.

All of these things, and so much more, make up our aesthetic which has an impact on our aura, which can signal to others if we can be trusted or respected. If people do not trust or respect us, trying to accomplish anything with them will be an uphill battle at best.

Being respected is helpful; however, the foundation of any successful relationship is built on trust. You can respect someone, but not trust them. You can even love someone, but not trust them. For example, if your son is a raging drug addict and is abusive, you might love him because he is your son, but not trust him. Or if your boss is the world's expert on a topic, you might highly respect her, but not trust her because she never gives you credit for the work you contribute to her or the team's success.

With trust, you can layer on the most difficult of scenarios, and you know all will be resolved. Trust allows for healthy conflict, buoys accountability, and promotes macromanagement. Unlike first impressions, trust must be earned. It can take years to gain it, yet seconds to lose it.

While we cannot change people's natural tendency to prejudge, we can show up in such a way that gives them the best sense of who we are which will then allow us the time to earn their trust and respect.

Cowboy-Conductor Challenge

Research shows that discriminatory judgment is due to the output of the nonconscious reflexive part of our brain that prefers fast and effortless thoughts. Here are some ways you can counter it.

Dress for success. As you get dressed in the morning, think carefully about the message you will be sending to those who you will meet that day. If you have a meeting where you need to show complete confidence, then perhaps choose the red tie. If you want to exude a calming vibe, throw on the blue dress. Choose every single piece of clothing, down to the pattern on your socks, with as much discrimination as will be foisted upon you by others.

Think before you speak. When speaking with others,

listen to the words you choose, the pitch and volume of your voice, the pace of your delivery. All of these will influence the reaction you get from those around you. Do you need to motivate someone? Then perhaps a higher pitch, louder volume, and quicker tempo might do the trick. Need to quickly defuse tensions? Try lowering your pitch, quieting your volume, and slowing your speed. Lastly, pretend you have a built-in time delay to catch words and phrases you do not want to wind up on primetime television. Always think a few steps ahead of what you are about to say. The words you choose and how you deliver them will forever be etched on one's heart. How do you feel your pitch, volume and tone are affecting others? Is it accomplishing what you had hoped or making things worse?

Pay attention to being at attention. Posture sends a message. It can be used to scare off a mountain lion or save yourself from a mother grizzly defending her cubs. Notice how you enter a room, greet an interviewer, or look on a video conference frame. How you pose not only signals to the world how you feel, but who you are.

So, dress the part, warm up your vocal chords, and "a-ten-hut!"

ON THE POWER OF EMPOWERMENT

Saddling Up

How many times have you marveled at powerful leaders, those who know what they want, know how to get it, and know how to convince others to do their bidding? Those who are admired have gained the trust and respect of others. Those who are not are usually the ones wielding their power around like a threatening stick as they try to coerce others into compliance. This kind of power is one that is feared, not revered. But what if you used power to allow others to do as they wish? Seems counterintuitive to claim power by giving it away. Right? Maybe not. Let's explore.

Conversation

Paul:

So, you mentioned that horses don't make decisions by emotions. But, if they don't make decisions by emotions, what do they do?

Dustin:

It's fight or flight for them. A horse looks at it in one of two ways.

My one mentor always says, "We've been eating horses longer than we've been riding them." Which is true. So you have to look at it from a horse's perspective. You get ready to do something new with that horse and in his mind, he might be thinking, "Is this the ritual they do just before they decide to put me on the spit and run me over the barbecue?!"

When I'm presenting something to the horse his reaction might be "this scares me" or "I'm unsure about this." In the wild when a horse feels scared or unsure he has the freedom to move his feet to a distance where he feels secure and then he will stop and turn around and he will look at whatever made him insecure or scared. Given time, usually his curiosity kicks in and that horse will come back to check out whatever it was.

With humans, when they start to present something to a horse, the horse might get scared, but instead of letting the horse move its feet in a way that the horse finds some relief and freedom through movement, they try and restrain the horse. Then the horse thinks they have to fight to save themselves because the human has left them no other options. So that's when it kicks or strikes or whatever it needs to do to save itself.

People need to learn to work in the middle of that, where that horse has the freedom to move and they're not confined to the point where they feel they need to fight. They figure out through movement there's comfort. The human can get a horse so terrified it just wants to run away, but the human should have backed off before it got to that point. Maybe one needs to stop and look at their presentation and address it another way so the horse doesn't feel like it needs to flee or fight for its life.

Paul:
Flight is the first instinct when a horse is scared of something, and fight is their second instinct?

Dustin:
Right.

Paul:
But we've learned in situations where there might be an active shooter that the best thing to do for human beings is to freeze, and then flight, and then fight. Stay there and freeze should be the first response for us. Do horses have that kind of freeze reaction?

Dustin:
Yes and no. A horse will flight before they will fight, and they'll try to escape anything that is harmful or anything that they feel is endangering them until they feel

comfortable. If they can't find a way to get away from it, then it will turn into more of a fight situation where they'll bite, kick, strike, or whatever else. Additionally, you'll find some of these horses that have been in programs and they've been pushed so hard that they freeze. You ask them to do something and they just stand there. They don't have a response because of how they have been trained up to that point or how they have been worked. No matter what they tried to do to please the human, it was never right. And so if they tried a flight, they got in trouble; if they fought, they got in trouble. So, pretty soon they learned to just stand there and take the beating, if you will, and pretty much freeze up. Those horses are really tough to get along with because with them less is really more, because you've got to find little things that they'll even attempt to do and then you build on that to get them to where they want to even try again. But it doesn't take much to crush them back to where they just don't want to do anything. So there's a little bit of a freezing there.

Paul:
So their freeze is them giving up.

Dustin:
Yes. And you'll see that sometimes when a horse has been, say, in the wild and they were in the band of horses and something comes up and attacks them such as a mountain lion, and they've run and the mountain lion has got a hold of them and they have fought and fought and fought, and, pretty soon, they just stand there. And that's when everything takes place. The killing happens. They just freeze, and that's what happens right before death. And so,

to them, that's the closest to being dead as they're going to be. What a shitty way to live your life having to live with that possibility. It's freeze and don't move; the end has caught up with you. Think about the instinct that's within a horse. Think about the feel that's within a horse. A horse can feel a fly land anywhere on their body in a thirty-mile-an-hour wind and they can swish their tail up there, and aim that tail just right to knock that fly off their hide. But if you beat on them and thump on them so hard, they just have no feel left to them, no flight, no fight, no nothing. I mean, God put so much in a horse, and for a human to take all that out of it, to have a horse just freeze up like that when asked to do something, that's a terrifying state of mind to have to live in.

I think that also goes back to self-preservation. Some horses have a whole lot more self-preservation than other horses. Some will fight to the death; others won't. A lot of that goes to the breeding and different things. A mustang is gonna push you a whole lot farther than a horse that was raised in a stall that has been handled by humans from the moment they hit the ground. Their flight and their fight is going to be in there, but it's just not going to be the same as a horse that's been left to his own devices. Self-preservation is very real within the horse. It is a very big driving force within a horse as to how they're going to respond to this stuff.

Paul:
Bringing it back to people, depending on how you were raised or how much adversity you faced perhaps equals how much perseverance you have saved up for the future whether for personal issues or professional work situations.

There are those people who give up pretty quickly, who haven't had a lot of adversity to toughen them up. This is probably not popular, but I believe this is part of the reason why some of the millennial generation who have been raised to get a gold star for just showing up, have a more difficult time with perseverance. And those who are more scrappy, maybe grew up on the streets, have a little more fight in them and a little more of this toughness.

Very interesting how a horse flees first and fights second whereas humans freeze first, flee second and fight last.

Dustin:
Well, the difference between humans and horses is you're looking at a predator versus prey. We're predators. Horses are prey. So there's going to be some differences there, but you can turn a horse into a predator. There's been people that have treated them bad enough that they're just like a predator. You walk into a stall and they come at you pawing, rearing up, striking, kicking, biting, whatever else. And it's a human who made that. That is not in a horse naturally. You can probably attest to this better, but there're humans that are that way too. There are humans that have been betrayed and reduced to prey animals and there are humans that have become aggressive predators.

Paul:
Yes, it goes back to their upbringing and their surroundings, and the environment that they grew up in.

Dustin:
It bothers me quite a bit because I see so many of these horses that live with so much trouble. A horse that has

trouble or anxiety in their life because they were treated by the human with harsh gimmicks and crap that people think they needed to get along with the horse instead of searching for a better way. It's like, to me, could you imagine living a life in that kind of fear? All the time? When they put a saddle on me, they're gonna jerk my head down and they're gonna kick me in the belly with those spurs, and it's going to be a bad day. I mean, can you imagine waking up every day? It'd be like a child waking up in a home where you get beat every day versus a child that is raised in an encouraging, loving home.

Paul:

I was thinking about that, and abusive relationships, and bullies at school and at work, and people who feel like they have to dominate to lead. In any of those situations, but especially in the workplace where you have leaders and followers, the leaders can't just drag their teams to their goals. There has to be a much more collaborative relationship, you know, a trusting and respectful relationship, but also a collaborative one.

So it feels like what you're saying about horses needing to feel that freedom is similar to people who want to feel in control of their own destiny. And we as leaders need to provide an environment that supports believing in that and exploring that, realizing that at the same time they have the space and expression to be free, there also have to be parameters. Whether at home, school, or work, there has to be some discipline within the freedom. So I think there has to be a mix of both, and you have to have not only the structure, but also the ability to operate within the grey within that structure.

Dustin:

Exactly. I say all the time what I picked up from my mentor, "The horse is entitled to his opinion." No different than you or I. It doesn't make the horse right, but the horse also needs to understand my opinion, and I will let the horse work at their opinion until they understand that their opinion is really not working and they find a way that mine does work.

Well, what I find with a lot of these people that are riding horses and hanging their shingle out as a trainer is they don't listen to the horse's opinion and they don't care. The human doesn't understand the horse is working through its opinion. The human automatically sees the horse as being disobedient when actually they need to see where the horse is coming from and stop and present what they want in a way that makes sense to the horse from where the horse is working from. So they run out of knowledge and they get barbaric and do things that they normally wouldn't do, or they get upset and start whipping on a horse to the point where the horse and them are now in a fight.

Well, I think it's the same thing in a lot of business-type settings where someone has moved up into a managerial position and they're not really sure and they don't have the information or the knowledge of how to keep that team moving forward so then they get to the point where they get hard on everybody and it just becomes a fight or flight deal where their opinions aren't respected. Their thoughts aren't respected, and it's like, just the heck with you, this is what needs to happen. Does that make sense to you?

Paul:

Absolutely. So when you're talking about those managers and the people who are abusing or not really addressing horses' needs properly, those are the owners, those are the other trainers you're talking about. So the horse aside, you're talking about developing the leaders, which would be either the owners or the trainers or whoever else works with horses in this way.

Have you had situations where you've had to work on the trainers? The horse owners? And how do you do that?

Dustin:

All the time. And honestly, it boils down to one thing: it has to come from inside them.

They can bring me a horse with any kind of problem and I can get to where I can get along with that horse. And I can send that horse home. And it'll take a week, a month, and they'll call saying that horse is doing the same thing again. But if the human didn't change what they were doing when they went back to working with their horse, they're going to fall into the same pattern.

It'd be like being in a relationship. And it's an abusive relationship. And they say they're going to change. You go through counseling, and you spend time apart, and you say everything's going to change when you get back home. And the first day you're home things are pretty good. And then the week rolls on, perhaps even two weeks, before something goes south. And then, badda-bing-badda-boom, somebody pops somebody and you're right back to where you started.

Both sides have to be willing to change.

Ray Hunt said it best, "You have to accept defeat in

order to gain success." Most people aren't willing to accept responsibility for why it didn't work with the horse. It takes them a while to finally say, "I need to try and do something else, something new to gain success with this horse."

Horses are so forgiving. They are the most noble creatures in the world to me. I don't have words to explain what horses mean to me and what they've done for me and how many I wished I could go back and rub because I didn't have the knowledge then that I have now. And I don't have now what I'll have in twenty years, and I'll spend the rest of my life searching for answers because I don't think this is anything I'm ever going to have all the answers to. It's a lifelong journey.

Paul:
How do you get the people over that hump in order to help their horse?

Dustin:
Usually, they'll bring me their horse and they tell me about all the bad stuff their horse does and everything else. And so with every month I have their horse, I'd give the owners three lessons or training free because I want that horse and them to be successful. It cuts into my bottom line, but, for me, it's about the horse. And so they come, they take their lessons, and they're supposed to be hour lessons but it usually runs about two hours because I'm trying to set them up for success at home the best I can. And every now and then, I'll get some that come in here and they want to come back every week and watch their horse, which is pretty good because they get to see a lot of things, they get

to experience a lot of things. They get to hear me talk about a lot of things that they need to hear. Those are usually the people that actually got it. And when they get home, I'll get pictures or I'll get e-mails, "Hey, look how great we're doing."

I try to send them home with the tools to be successful. I have to go in there and really reintroduce the owners to what's going on and change *their* habits. Because it's the human I've got to change. And it's pretty tough because it's really easy to fall into old habits. Old habits are hard to break, but you gotta have that *want* to get along better and do better. That's something I'm always trying to instill in people. My whole life I've always wanted to do better. And to me, it's not about showing horses. As Ray Hunt always said, "My goal with the horse is not to beat someone else, it's to win within myself." It's about beating what I can do with my horse. I don't need someone else to judge me and my horse and say, "Oh, you did a good job. Here is a blue ribbon." That doesn't matter to me. To me, it's how happy and how satisfied my horse is with how we're getting along. That's the reward to me. If I walk to the barn and my horse knickers at me as I walk in the barn, by God, we've got a pretty good thing going.

Paul:
That's very true. All of what you said is really insightful. Again, in the workplace, where you have managers or leaders who may call you in as a consultant and say, "Fix this team. This team is just not working. It's not performing. I need them fixed. Go take them off-site. Do some retreats." Yet, the leader doesn't go on the retreat. They stay at work. And as you said, it's really the leader

that needs the fixing because the employees are reacting to the leader's leadership.

Same as you, I can very much sense the minute I walk into a healthy organization because I can't tell the difference between who's in the C-Suite, who's in middle management or who's just starting because everyone feels a collective ownership. A personal ownership. And, that's very different than "You are my employees, and I am your leader" approach, which is what you have been talking about.

Dustin:

I am the leader, but I work harder on building a partnership with the horse. One built on trust and respect that leads to a union where the horse can sense what I need before I ask for it, and it becomes ninety percent mental and just ten percent physical.

Until you've felt that, you don't have a clue what a horse can do for you. I mean, it's something that once you get a taste of it, man, it's something you're chasing the rest of your life. It is the most phenomenal feeling to be sitting on a horse knowing that you need to turn over there to cut that cow, and as you start to think it, that horse just rolls right out there and makes the stop. The horse will fill in and help you so much. And the horse becomes your best friend.

If you can get people to work for you the way that horse will work for you when you have that partnership, you'll have them for a lifetime.

Paul:
Yeah, that's exactly on point. I often talk to leaders about building a racehorse team for that reason. If you have a racehorse team, you don't need to beat them. You know they're going take care of themselves. They know how they need to support you and support each other, and they don't need to be micromanaged. I think that instinct certainly applies to the workplace, and it also appears in personal relationships where you complete each other's sentences and are thinking the same thing at the same time or understanding what the other person needs without having to say anything because you've gotten more intuitive and you've built that unspoken relationship that you can't teach. Actually, I guess you can teach it, but it's really learned through interactions over time and then building that trust.

Dustin:
Yep, good judgment comes from experience, and experience comes from bad judgment in life.

Paul:
Right. *The pond of life.*

Dustin:
Exactly. It's just how it all works. It's interesting to me, because as I was writing this down there were so many things that came to my head that tied everything together

in business, and in life, and in horses. I think about it all the time.

Working with horses makes other areas of your life better that don't even pertain to horses. You don't realize it, because you learn so much. You learn empathy. There's so many things that you learn through this. It's amazing. And the coolest part about the whole deal is you have a conversation every day and you never speak a word.

Paul:

Since we're talking about cowboys and conductors, there are a lot of nonverbal, empowerment signals that go on between conductors and the musicians who are in front of them.

Musicians, and you can help me translate it horse-wise, have their own ideas, just like horses do. And they believe they know what's right and what's wrong. They've got sort of a black-and-white mentality even though they're artistic. They ponder, "Is that the right way to play that phrase? Is that the right way to interpret this piece of music?" And it's not good or bad and they're not right or wrong, but they're very opinionated. Most of them, by the time they get to the concert stage, have probably spent the majority of their life in their craft. It's not like, "I will go to college, and maybe by the time I'm finishing my master's degree I'll figure out what I'm going do, and then I'm going to pick up the violin." It doesn't work that way. You usually start by the time you're six or seven if you're going to be a professional, if not earlier. So it's something that is almost inbred, I guess, like a horse's instincts and actions.

And so when you are a guest conductor for the first

time, it's challenging. When an orchestra works with their permanent music director and they see that person week after week, month after month, year after year, they develop that special relationship you talk about. But there are a lot of times where they also have guest conductors come up in front of the orchestra, not their regular leader, just somebody who's coming into town for a week. And as a guest conductor you basically have three to four rehearsals, depending on the situation, of about two and a half hours each to put together a full concert program. As a guest conductor, if you've never met the orchestra, you have less than four minutes, if that, to make an impression on that herd of musicians as to whether they're going to follow you or not. This is related to what we discussed in our trust, respect, and first impressions conversation earlier.

Even though I am no longer a conductor, I use many of the techniques that I learned in music school. What my conducting teachers would always say is, "Show it. Don't say it." You can have a lot of nonverbal communication and even very intimate, one-on-one communication with the musicians in the orchestra if you know how to focus your attention and focus those nonverbal communication signals. As a matter of fact, it can also go badly. I had a conducting colleague who had this very intense look all the time. It didn't mean anything, but he just looked at a player so intensely that they would frighteningly say, "What did I do?" And he would say, "It's nothing, I just really love your playing!" He was very intense and very passionate. But the other person didn't take it that way. So it's not only about non-verbal, it's also making sure it's the correct nonverbal. And with orchestras time is money. If you stop the music, you better have something to say that's valuable and succinct.

So I'm talking about how, like you with horses, it's very similar to a conductor's approach to musicians and working with them in a way that's not forcing them. That force used to be the way of the dictator conductor who worked with orchestras decades ago. But in the last twenty or so years, it's much more collaborative. And now it's about riding that herd together not only as a coach, but also as a partner using the power of empowerment.

When you train and ride horses, you're not their dictator. You're their coach, their partner, in some sense, right?

Dustin:

Oh yeah, totally. And it's interesting that you say that because, for example, let's take a group of colts we're going to start. Each colt you work with is a new personality and you have to present yourself in a way that fits that horse. As you go through the bunch, it's different for each colt to get them ready to saddle. Some colts are really troubled about it and some aren't. But once you have all of them saddled, you may turn them all out together in a pen. Then you may go out on horseback and move the colts around allowing them to move their feet and get comfortable with the saddle.

And so that would be like the conductor first coming out there with all the colts. It's the first time they've all had the saddle on so they're all crashing and banging into each other and stirrups are flopping and the horses aren't sure what's going where. And I'm sure it might be kind of like an orchestra where notes are flying everywhere, and it's kinda not in unison yet. Similar with horses. They'll move around there for a while in each direction and you'll change directions and cut them back through the middle and pretty soon, within a little bit of time, that whole herd of horses will be falling on the same foot at the same time. It'll all be in unison. All their front feet will land at the same time coming around the corner. All will strike the hind at the same time. I mean, it will all turn into unison as a herd of horses. At one point, one colt might get troubled with the saddle and buck throwing the cadence of the herd off. The guy on horseback might have to help that horse with getting going again until it's found its way through the trouble and can move out softly with the herd. And I can't help but think it's probably the same as putting an orchestra together and seeing how all that different stuff can slowly come together and turn into a beautiful, magical thing. There's nothing cooler than seeing twenty-five head of horses that have been bouncing around, carrying on like a bunch of broncs, come together in one fluid motion and you've got all those feet moving in the same cadence. It's knowing that all those horses are let down and not troubled at that moment. So, to me, it's like the rhythm in a concert it just hits you somewhere deep inside.

Paul:
Exactly. I have that same feeling, yet it's not a feeling of power. It's a feeling of accomplishment, a feeling of,

"Wow, all these powerful horses, or all these powerful musicians, trusted each other and trusted me to do that." The power of empowerment, it's the stuff goose-bumps are made of.

Dustin:

It's amazing to see all of that come together and for them to put that trust in there. I mean, to me, it's almost a sign of gratitude to a point where the horse lets down and relaxes and thinks, "I can just move out." Because if one of them horses is a little bit tight, it'll cause the other horses around him to all fall out of that same cadence, and then everything will fall out of order again.

Paul:

The same thing happens on stage. There can be one musician who comes in at the wrong time, and can throw eighty other people off, almost like a ripple effect. However, humans can learn to correct this problem quickly when that happens. But if people aren't aware that it's happening, it takes longer to correct and more damage will be done. It is a very similar thing that you're talking about.

Yelling at people that they're wrong or they were out of tune or they have the wrong rhythm doesn't help. It's much better to say, "How about if we try it this way?" or,

"This might sound better if you phrase it this way," as opposed to, "That was shitty!"

There has to be tremendous respect for the talent that's on that stage and a tremendous respect for the power of that horse or that herd as opposed to, "I am the conductor, I am the trainer, and you must obey me." That doesn't work for all the reasons you mentioned.

Dustin:

Well, I tell a lot of people I don't really like the phrase training horses. If I was talking to most people and I said, "Hey, you're going to start training," what's the first thought that comes to your mind when you talk about training? You think about school; it's gonna be hard work and you're going to have to exert yourself. It's going to be like going to the gym. I have to run or something. It's going to be all of this hard work. We don't train our children for life. We teach our children. We set them up for success. We provide them with provisions. We help them. We guide them. We structure it so that they learn. So, to me, it's trying to teach these horses what the human's idea is, instead of train them. I don't want my horse to be a machine that I get on and pull levers. If I wanted that, I'd drive a damn tractor. That's not what I want to do. So, to me, it's a teaching deal to where we work in unison. I would assume being a conductor, getting your musicians to perform in that manner, would be a lot the same way because you're going to set them up for the best success that you can so that when you get up there it all flows together in unison.

Paul:

Exactly! Because the musicians don't need training either. They don't even need teaching. What you're sharing with them is a different perspective. Quite frankly, that's what art and music is. It's an interpretation. It's a perspective. It's not right; it's not wrong. It's your version of the world that you want to share with others. You hope you can convince your orchestra, and ultimately your audience, of your vision. Because they have to believe in your interpretation, your story, what you're selling them, so to speak, what you're trying to encourage them to adopt. And if they don't believe it, or they understand it but your ideas are too far from normal, then there can be a revolution. That said, the great orchestras will still perform brilliantly for you onstage at the concert even if they don't agree with your interpretation, but all the way up to that point you're dragging them, kicking and screaming. It's not a pretty situation.

Dustin:

That's interesting that you say that because everything that we're teaching the horse to do are all moves the horse makes every day on its own. All we're asking them to do is make those movements under us when we ask for them so we can work in unison where the horse and the rider become one.

Paul:

Through empowerment.

Connecting the Dots

Horses are powerful creatures. Yet, our instinct has been to control their energy rather than allow them to use it freely as we teach them. We have all kinds of gadgets and techniques to coerce. Why? Because it is faster and easier to whip it and kick it than to build a partnership. But in the end, is the horse doing what you want because it trusts and respects you? No. Instead, it is reacting to your discipline out of fear, hoping that if it does as you command, you will let it live to see the next day. Same goes for humans. In the workplace, we threaten by withholding that promotion unless..., or firing unless..., or chastising you among your peers unless.... Does that seem like an environment in which you would like to spend every day, every week, every year until you retire? No, of course not! Yet this is happening in organizations all over the world.

We tend to believe that power is control, so without it we assume that we are out of control, that we are not in complete control of the situation or of the people who report to us. However, wielding power over people produces the opposite result. It tends to shut people down, and over time it causes them to freeze, just like horses. Freezing equals resignation. Death. Leading a department of people who have given up is not the definition of being in control of the situation, because that one-sided power has caused them to give up. Try accomplishing your annual goals within *this* scenario.

What if we shifted our thinking around power

dynamics? In Kenneth Blanchard's book *Empowerment Takes More Than a Minute*, he writes, "Empowerment is not giving people power, people already have plenty of power, in the wealth of their knowledge and motivation, to do their jobs magnificently. We define empowerment as letting this power out." Just as convincing a horse by letting it move its feet, to feel in control of its destiny, one can unleash the power that is already within those we lead by creating an owner-operated environment where they have both the responsibility and the authority to do their job, one in which they feel personally compelled, as an owner does, for the success of the company. Now, try accomplishing your annual goals within *this* scenario.

Which approach do you prefer? Hopefully, it is a no-brainer.

Cowboy-Conductor Challenge

How do you begin to empower people? You cannot just say, "Now you are empowered. Go forth!" As Blanchard states, it "takes more than a minute."

Start by blocking out a few hours on the calendar to gather those who report to you and perhaps even some of those who report to them. Choose a topic to brainstorm. This could be a new initiative, an ongoing challenge, or perhaps the future strategic direction of the organization. Note that asking for people's opinions is not enough. Your approach and reaction to their suggestions will determine when and if they feel comfortable moving into an empowered state of mind and action. Set the game rules to allow everyone to be vulnerable. One could be "there is no such thing as a stupid idea." If they are shy at first, you may need to start with a really outrageous idea to show that no idea is a bad one.

Once your team gets on a roll with suggestions, write them all down on big Post-it® note sheets around the room so at the end of the meeting everyone can see what they have accomplished as well as feel they have been heard. Just like Dustin does when working with young colts, let this first exchange of ideas be enough for the moment. Let them run free. Thank everyone for their openness and participation.

Next, set a follow-up meeting to review all of the ideas and begin finding themes and drilling down on those that seem particularly exciting and doable. Have your team break out into smaller groups that are self-guided and allow them to pick a theme to tackle. Have them come up with the goals, strategies, tactics, timelines, and the people who will be held accountable for the idea's successful implementation. Finally, allow them to execute on those initiatives that everyone believes will move the organization forward.

How did that feel to empower your team? Did you feel stronger as a leader or weaker? How did your team feel? Did they feel they engaged or micromanaged?

According to numerous surveys, more than compensation, employees value working for an organization where they feel they are truly making a contribution. Why not capitalize on this?

ON DISCRIMINATING LEADERSHIP

Saddling Up

Seldom are there words that, by their very definitions, have polar opposite connotations. Discriminate is one of them. On the one hand, it means to make an unjust or prejudicial distinction, and on the other, it means to recognize a distinction, to be able to differentiate. It is within the latter meaning that we describe discriminating leadership. As your world view and engagement of everyone in it continues to expand, you must fine-tune your ability to see everyone as who they are and not cast judgment based on biases or a generalized understanding of people. Our focus is on what each person brings to the success of the organization, and to each other, no matter what their professional position or personal journey.

Conversation

Paul:

A similarity between horses and humans is that, in their natural state, they both live in groups. Horses in herds and humans in one form of a community or another. Within this structure, horses have what you have told me is a *herd mentality*. What exactly, from a layman's point of view, is herd mentality?

Dustin:

Well, it's a very sophisticated structured system. There's always a lead mare, and she's always going to be the leader of the bunch. Everybody thinks there's a stud horse in there, and that he's the lead. No, he gets dumped on all year long 'til breeding season comes around, and then he gets others' attention, if you know what I mean.

It's a very structured hierarchy as to how things fall into place, where each stands. You can probably relate this to the business side of things. You've got your lead mare and she's the CEO of the company. And then you've got your vice president, and then you've got your secretary, and so on. It's the same thing in the herd, and you go all the way down to your worker bees. Now, with that being said, it's not like the CEO lead mare just stands around and does nothing all day. She's grazing. She's producing babies. She's doing everything that everybody else is doing, but she's in charge. If things start to happen that need her attention, she'll find her way back to the herd, and she'll lead everybody to wherever they need to go. It's a very structured deal. When they go to the water hole, she'll drink first. When they feed, she'll eat first. It's very structured in how it works. If a horse steps out of line, she'll pin an ear, she'll dive at them and bare her teeth, whatever else it takes to move that other horse and send the message, "No you get back in line and stay in your structured place," which is very much what our society needs to do right now with everything going on.

Horses have been roaming the Earth longer than we have, and, as I've said before, we've been eating them longer than we've been riding them. And that herd mentality hasn't changed. They've been around millions of years, and it hasn't changed. It's still the same today as it was clear back then. They've evolved, but they've evolved for the better. I'm not saying we haven't evolved for the better, but if we're not careful, we're not gonna evolve for the better. But they haven't changed their structured hierarchy because it works. It keeps things in order. There's a very strict order of how things go and how things play out.

We spoke the other day about people with special needs. They would still be accepted into that herd, as part of that herd. The horses wouldn't discriminate and say, "Oh well, you've got a need so you're on your own." The herd would band together, and they would take care of it. If it's an older horse that's not getting on well, with time that horse is going to move out of that herd and let nature take its course.

Paul:

Talking about discrimination. Do horses discriminate based on the color of their coat or the kind of class of horse they are or anything like that? Is there any sort of shunning of horses?

Dustin:
Not really. We've got the minis. We've got the ponies and full-size horses. And there's not a shunning of any of them. You can

put mini horses out with big horses. You know, at first, they'll think, "Holy Hell, there's a really small animal out here! What are you?" But the little horse just wants to be the same as the big horse so pretty soon they will all run together and get along just fine. There's not a shunning because it's a mini horse or that horse is chestnut or that horse is grey or he's a paint horse instead of a bay horse. There's none of that. You look at a herd of horses out running wild, there could be every color under the sun. There's no discrimination in any way.

Paul:
What about male or female discrimination?

Dustin:
There's none.

Paul:
They're equal?

Dustin:

Everyone's welcome. The only thing you find, and it's not discrimination, is each band of mares will have only one mature stud horse, but every spring you could have the young stud colts coming around that may challenge that stud for his band of mares. And maybe there will be a little contest to see who will get that band of mares. And then there's times that the old horse gets whipped and the younger one moves in, but that's the evolution of things and then you get something new into their breeding program. That's just God's way of saying, "Hey, we can't have the same horse breeding the same herd forever." So it's a structured environment.

Paul:

What's interesting to me is that we tend to prefer an egalitarian society, and yet you said the herd mentality is a structured hierarchy. I think we tend to confuse those things as humans by insisting that everyone's equal; therefore, everyone has an equal voice and an equal position. As a matter of fact, one challenge I discovered with a recent client of mine was that they wanted everyone to be equal, to have the same voice. They wanted everyone to be in the same line of reporting, not reporting up, not reporting down. There was no, what I call, "hierarchy of decision making" or "decision matrix." There was a lot of discussion, but no one person ultimately made the decision or was held accountable, and so they flatlined as an organization. If all the horses are non-discriminate and they're equal, so to speak, yet you talk about a structured hierarchy - how does that work? How does this philosophy of "it doesn't matter whether you're male, female, whether you're small, large, or different colors because everyone's equal, everyone's treated equally" coexist within a hierarchical structure? It's a hierarchical structure of what?

Dustin:
The herd dynamic.

Paul:
What determines the hierarchical structure and what purpose does it serve to have a hierarchy? Do horses make decisions?

Dustin:
They make a lot of decisions that you don't think about. They make a decision if we're gonna go to the north to follow feed today or if we're gonna go to the south. If the wind is blowing, are we going to turn our hind ends to it or are we going to turn our heads to it? There's all kinds of decisions always being made. But your lead mare, she's going to probably be your toughest horse. She's going to be, what we would say in our society, the most opinionated. And she's going to be the most aware, if you will. Whoever is at the bottom is probably not going to be the most aware or the toughest; they'll probably be the first one to get eaten when the coyotes or the mountain lions show up, because they're just not going to be as aware and sensitive. So it plays into what the animals' traits are as to where they fall in the hierarchy.

Paul:
So degrees of awareness is what decides the structure?

Dustin:

Well, there's some degrees of awareness. There's some degrees of personality. You know, some horses are more pushy; some horses are a lot more soft and they'll let other horses push them around. Just like some people steamroll over people and other people find themselves being other people's doormats.

I often tell my clients, "When you go to the grocery store, I want you to walk down the aisle with your shopping cart and see what happens. Because I'll bet you a $100 that when someone comes at you, you step to the side." "Well, yeah, I always do," they'll say. That's interesting because I go down through the aisles and see how many of *them* I can move. Not because I'm being rude. Just to me, it's "do I move their feet or do they move mine?" And it's real interesting because you'll be going down through there and you can tell so much about a person's personality just in the shopping store. I do it all the time. It drives Aimee up the wall.

Paul:

I'm going to try that.

Dustin:

Now granted, I'll see an elderly lady come in, and of course I'll get out of her way. But I'll see some kid coming and he's strolling down through there and he thinks he's pretty tough, and I just keep on watching, and pretty soon he's moved ten or twelve people. He just steamrolled them out of the way. However, he meets up with me and he dives over to the side. And I chuckle and walk on by. Then I see somebody else come in. I can tell that they're the one who always steps out of everybody's way, so I'll just move out of their way and let them go by. Well, they'll just smile and perk right up and you can almost see their whole demeanor lift up. Now that's a separate thing from what we're just talking about, but it's an interesting little project that I have people do because it shows them a lot about themselves, that they are unaware of what they usually do.

So when it comes to the horse, horses read body language. For example, you're in the round pen with your horse and, as we're talking, the horse steps in closer to you. You rub him and then you step away from him and he steps towards you again. When you step away from him you are teaching him to walk on you, that he moves your feet. If he were in a herd of horses and you were the lead horse, you would have pinned an ear when he first approached. If he didn't respond, next you might have dove at him and bit him. If he still didn't get the point you may haul off and double-barrel him with both hind feet as to say, "Get the hell back!" He'd learn right there not to challenge you as the lead horse. So right then, it's done. It's settled. That's it. You taught him his boundaries. Horses don't just go around picking fights. It's not who they are or what they do. Horses don't like trouble. They try and stay out of trouble. And, we as humans, we tend to fall into trouble quite a bit.

Paul:
So this hierarchy is degrees of awareness, personality, posture, and even presence. Correct?

Dustin:
Oh yeah.

Paul:

Not only presence of posture, but being present, as in focus. It's not like in packs of coyotes where the weakest links are the lowest on the chain and can possibly get eaten. You're talking about a more sophisticated hierarchy.

Dustin:

Yeah, whoever's the weakest link on there is going to get eaten, of course, because they're going to be the slowest. They're going to be the slowest to react and everything else. But the difference in my mind, and I could be wrong on this, but my opinion, in a coyote pack, the weakest one is likely to go. They'll pick on him and he will fall off on his own. And that seems to be the demise of that coyote. However with horses, when one horse gets sick then pretty soon the whole herd gets sick because that one got sick and stayed with his herd. I mean they stay together through pretty much everything, and are always looking out for each other unlike coyotes. When something's not quite right coyotes show their predator side. They kick whatever's bad out and it'll get eaten, but it doesn't seem to be that way with horses. There's a significant difference between predator and prey.

Paul:

It's interesting because, as we discussed earlier, I wish we as humans had more of this structured, yet egalitarian situation where there's a significant degree of responsibility within the herd mentality.

I think that's what we strive for in the workplace when we talk about what I call a culture of ownership or an "owner-operated culture" where the CEO all the way down to the front-line people all feel equally responsible for the organization and that their opinions are heard, that what they say matters. And, yet, there still is that hierarchical structure, that decision matrix that I mentioned earlier where there have to be decisions made at some point even if everyone gets to weigh in with their opinion. Without that decision matrix, we get to a point where everyone equally has an opinion, but then there is no one to make the decision, no one to be held accountable.

Using discriminating leadership allows us to work through these tricky situations.

Dustin:
On the orchestra side of things, there's got to be somewhat of a structured hierarchy as to what's what, whether it be in the violins, or the brass or the drums or whatever section it may be. I'm sure there's a hierarchy as to who's the top. I could be wrong, but if you watch an orchestra, there are several musicians playing the violin. I gotta think one of them has to be better than the rest of them.

Paul:
Well, yes and no. In an ideal situation, everyone should be equal even though they have different parts to play, so to speak. While you have two sections of violins, first violins and second violins, it's not that one is a less important group of players than the other. They have different parts to play that are complementary. They have different positions in the company, as it were. In the most perfect situation, and I'm not saying this always happens, everyone should be of equal expertise and skill level. Like I said before, ideally, it'd be great to have a racehorse team

where everyone has similar levels of experience, similar levels of talent.

Going back to that decision matrix, in an orchestra, if the oboe player asks, "Maestro, can we try it this way instead?" a healthy enough ego and a respect for that musician and their expertise would have the maestro respond with, "Sure let's try it your way and see how it works." But at the end of the day, it is the conductor who has the final decision and says, "Yes, we'll go with that" or "No, we're going to do it the way I wanted it the first time." I think this is where companies can really learn from this model. You have extremely talented musicians with decades of experience in front of you. Why not listen to them? Why not take their opinion and see if that makes it better or not? But at the end of the day, the conductor is the final decision maker, and they all know that.

But you don't have to beat them over the head with that decision-making power. You can have a lot of different opinions and still have everyone collaborate and feel they have contributed something to the final direction. That said, with an orchestra, you have eighty musicians on stage so you're not going to please every single person, because there are simply too many differing opinions. Nonetheless, you should still utilize the talent that you have in front of you and make decisions together keeping in mind that time is money. Any time you stop and discuss something it's costing you time and inevitably you're paying for that time even though they're not playing. You're still paying them to sit there and discuss your idea. So there are not a lot of discussions or a lot of long-drawn-out conversations about how the music should be interpreted or how the rehearsal should proceed, but there is still some of that.

Dustin:

So then, what is the difference between the first section versus the second section of the violins? What puts one in which section? How does that play out?

Paul:

It depends on a number of things. It depends on the sound that the music director wants to achieve. They usually play different parts. While both tend to play the melody, the second violins often play a supporting role as the harmony or counterpoint to the first violins. Additionally, in the time of Mozart and earlier, the two violin sections would sit on opposite ends of the stage, across from each other to create an echo effect. Often, you'll hear a phrase here and then it'll be mimicked over there. You can hear, and even see, that back-and-forth approach. You need those two sections to hear that stereophonic sound. So, one isn't inferior.

Dustin:

In all aspects of it then, your conductor, your maestro, is really your lead horse. And all those musicians play just as an important part as does the rest of the herd. I'm not saying that their opinions won't be heard or they can't move around or move their way through, but at the end of the day it takes the whole company just like it takes the whole herd for them to function together.

Paul:

Exactly right. And what's interesting as we're talking and you're mentioning the second versus first violin, is that there also is a first oboe and second oboe, sometimes also a third oboe part. Same goes with the flutes, horns, and trumpets. The third trumpet is no less important than the first trumpet, but they all have different parts to play. I remember when I used to conduct youth orchestras, the parents would get so upset that their kid was fourth horn or second oboe. They are all just as important. Do not get caught up on the number or the seat position. We can't all be the first oboe or we'd have eighty oboes! That wouldn't be very pleasing to an audience.

Going back to the herd mentality and an egalitarian model, I'd bet that halfway down the chain those horses aren't upset. They're doing their part. They're having fun. Given what you've been telling me, they probably don't wish they were ten horses up in the structure. What's interesting is, as humans, we create these barriers and create these frustrations for ourselves as opposed to just saying, "I'm just happy to have a job or be playing in the orchestra at all." We get caught up in our positions so much that it freezes us; it paralyzes us or it frustrates us. So we tend to approach life with a, "Well, since I'm only the fourth horn, I'm just going to give a fourth of a damn" mentality.

Dustin:

It makes me wonder with the human why we get so hung up on titles. Two quotes have always stuck out in my mind. Ray Hunt always said, "It takes a lifetime to learn to live a lifetime," and there's a lot to be said about that. And then, Dave Weaver says, "A guy can figure a lot of this out on his own, but why not learn from someone who has been there before and save yourself a lot of time and mistakes." Those two phrases are just embedded in my mind because I try and take what my mentors have given me; it saves me a lot of time and headaches. And I have found it has helped me advance farther because I haven't reproduced their mistakes. Even with that being said, a guy has to make some mistakes of his own. I have no problem picking up the phone and calling my mentors when I'm at an impasse, saying "Hey, this is where I'm at. I'm stuck." And they'll tell me, "Well try this, it's what worked for me." And throughout that exchange, we also get to build comradery. And if people would get along like that, things would be so much easier.

Paul:

It comes down to ego and misplaced pride. People feel they don't need someone else's opinion, that they're smart enough and can go do everything themselves. But not having an ego isn't healthy either. Everyone needs a nicely balanced, healthy ego. You should have enough of an ego to make decisions and move forward, but not such a big ego that it gets in the way of your decision-making and pisses off everyone else. And I agree with what you said about your mentors. My philosophy is, "If you have everything in life figured out, I really don't want to be a part of that." I don't trust anybody who's got life all figured out. I don't trust them at all. So many people seem to be in control of their every second. They believe they know everything about life.

Dustin:

People do that all the time with me. They'll say, "This is what you need to do with my horse and blah, blah, blah...." And I think, "Well, if you knew what needed to be done, why are you here? If you've got it all figured out, why do you need me?" Because if I ever think I've got it all figured out, I will quit doing what I'm doing because you can never stop learning. The horse always has something to teach you. It takes a lifetime to learn to live a lifetime.

Paul:

That is exactly what is at the heart of discriminating leadership. Every situation is unique. Not recognizing this is what gives consultants a bad reputation. Those con-sultants who have come up with a solution that has worked for them in a certain situation and then use it indiscriminately. In-stead of truly approaching every client's challenges with open eyes, they say,

"Well, that's this kind of problem, so here's the solution I've used before." You may have your bag of tricks that you've gained over life. I'm not saying that you don't use that bag, but you shouldn't immediately apply a solution before you've really dug into what the problem is.

What I've done in my career is to be really hands-on and approach every new problem with fresh eyes. I have a toolbox that I can draw from, but I don't get my tools out and start hammering on something before I know what the problem is. Does this sound similar to your approach?

Dustin:

Absolutely. I do it all the time. And people do the same thing with horses. They train one way and that's the only way they know how to do it. However, if it's not working, try something else - think outside the box. But they cannot do that. Maybe if you change one little thing up or you present it in a slightly different way, it might work like a charm. And I'm sure it's the same with conducting - you're doing it this way and the oboe player says "Let's try it that way." And you say, "Wow, that really rolled off a whole lot better and it sounded prettier so we're going take your suggestion." You thought outside the box and you did something different. You interpreted it one way; someone else interpreted differently than you did and look what it did to improve things. People get so close-minded and stuck in their ways. I agree with you 110%. They get so stuck on that one thing and they don't know how to do anything else. They are not using their discriminating leadership to do a work-around.

Paul:

And that oboe example I mentioned earlier is also about insecurity. If you're the conductor, you're the maestro. Do you allow yourself, in front of the entire orchestra, to acknowledge that the oboist had the solution?

If you're insecure, you don't let them own that solution even though you know it's better. You'll say it really didn't sound great even though the other seventy-nine musicians thought to themselves, "Sounded good to me. Actually, it was much better." But an insecure person wouldn't allow someone else to step into the leadership role, even for a second.

That's why I believe that the people with over-the-top egos are usually the ones who are the most insecure so they surround themselves with what I call an "asshole barrier" which repels everyone else to not even *think* about stepping into that leadership role.

Dustin:

I agree with you because I've seen that a lot in the horse world. There's been some people I followed and their egos are just out of this world, and they've said and done things that they say they'll never do and they do it. And I don't go for that stuff. I'm very, very critical about who I'll take information from and what I'll put in my chest that I want to use or in my toolbox, if you will. And, it's real interesting, because, most of the time when people say, "Well, who do you go ride with?" I'll think, "The people I ride with are on a level which you'll never understand. You wouldn't understand what they're trying to offer." The ones that I've surrounded myself with: Dave and Gwen, Buster, Lee; there is no ego there. They're really good at what they do, all of them, but they're just like you and me. They sit down and have a conversation with you. They sit down and have a whiskey with you, or whatever, have dinner. You'd think you're sitting there with a bunch of friends. You wouldn't know that you're sitting there with some of the people that are the most talented under the sun at what I do.

Paul:

And they don't have to prove anything to you. That reminds me of what you said the other day which is "I don't need to go and show horses." That's a healthy ego. You know what you know. You know what you don't know. You know what you want to learn. You don't need to have someone else validate that.

Dustin:

Exactly.

Paul:

You are your own competition. You can discriminate. You are your own best or worst enemy when it comes to criticism, right?

Dustin:

Correct. As Ray Hunt says, "My goal with the horse is not to beat someone, it is to win within myself."

Paul:

I think those who are comfortable in that and feel OK in that space are the ones who are the most down to earth because they are secure in themselves. They haven't figured out the entire world. They know there's a big world out there. Whatever the structure is of the universe, they know we are all just a tiny piece of it. You are not the end all be all of whatever your expertise or experience is.

Dustin:

Exactly, because if there's one thing I've learned, it's when you think you know it all, someone's gonna come around and they're going to show you that you don't. It's gonna happen. I've seen it time and time again in life, and so...

Paul:

...so save yourself the embarrassment and don't be an ass in the meantime.

Connecting the Dots

Imagine a world where everyone is equal, there is no discrimination, and all that you are judged on is your awareness, personality, posture, and presence. That is what is happening in the horse herd. They see past gender, color, type, size, age, and even health. None of that matters to them. While this egalitarian model has a hierarchy built into it, the inner-self, or inner-horse, is what makes the chain of command successful.

When we, as humans, think about leadership, we often think about position, stature, or tenure. We do not think about each person's individual contribution to the success of a project or organization. However, as leaders, we should fully know and appreciate every single person we work with or lead. In the ideal, no one person within a team should be more important than the others. Discriminating leadership is identifying and celebrating the internal qualities of each team member. Titles should not matter. Hierarchy should not matter. Longevity should not matter. What should matter is what each brings and how they bring it. In an orchestra, every musician has an individual part to play. The conductor, through discriminating leadership, must tap into each performer's awareness, personality, posture, and presence, in order to get all eighty virtuosos to play as one. If we viewed every person, in every position, as critical to an organization's success, imagine what could be accomplished.

Discriminating leaders must have curiosity, humility,

and a centeredness to them. Those who excel at discriminating leadership also possess a healthy ego. An ego that is large enough to "move" people, but small enough to keep them from being an ass. It is a delicate balance for sure.

Cowboy-Conductor Challenge

The fastest way to build your discriminating leadership muscles is to implement any one of these variations on the theme of musical chairs.

Boss for a day. Once a month, randomly draw a name from all of your direct reports or from all of the staff if the organization is small enough. Have that person assume the responsibility of boss, or leader of the department, for the day. Let him or her make any decision they feel is appropriate. Be sure to give them a few days before acting in the role to prepare for it however they wish. They might want to pick your brain about the role. They may want to read the job description. They may want to talk to the other direct reports. This alone will give you insight as to who they are and how they approach their work. Be sure to have that person report back about their experience, along with you, to the group.

Role reversal. Have everyone in the department or organization switch places for the day. This might be tricky if there are specifics to a person's job that cannot be learned overnight. If this is the case, then have the person in the specialty job teach the other for a few days. The humility it takes to learn the job will be well worth it. Have everyone report back to the group about their experience.

Shadowing. Have one person job-shadow another for the day. During that time the person being shadowed should explain what is happening, why decisions are being made the way they are, and what it takes to do the job. Again, have everyone report back to the group about their experience.

A completely different exercise, but effective one, is what we call *The A-hole Bowl*™. It is inspired by Robert I. Sutton's Harvard Business Review essay-turned-book titled, *The No Asshole Rule*. The premise is that, while you may be an absolute genius at your craft, if you are a jerk, we do not want to work with you because we have a culture of collaboration. Here is how you play the game. Start on a Monday, or the first day of your work week. Give each person one container and a bunch of poker chips that must be brought to every meeting. Any time someone thinks another is a jerk in a meeting, or while passing in the hall or via email, that person must toss one poker chip into that jerk's container. The person at the end of the week with the most chips is assigned a chore as punishment, such as cleaning the breakroom every day for a week. After a few cleanings, you might find the A-hole attitude drop precipitously amongst the team. If nothing else, their attentiveness to their verbal and physical cues, and the cues of others, will have dramatically increased.

Any of these exercises will give you and your team a taste of what it is like to be in the others' shoes. Discriminating leadership requires empathy and understanding of those in your care. Walking in their footsteps is one way to meet them where they are.

ON POTENTIAL

Saddling Up

Potential. While it is powerful, it is not the present. It is the future. Not what is, but what could be. It is what is possible. But, it is also scary. Do you have it? Will you live up to it? Can others see it in you? Are you able to discover it in others? A great deal of responsibility and experience is required when working with potential. In order to actualize what is possible, you have to be aware of what stands between you and your potential. What do you currently have in your tool kit to catch it, and what will you need to have in order to command it?

Conversation

Paul:

We've talked a lot about being in the moment as a leader, but we also have to think about the future. Take your young daughter. Think about how you're going to impact the future by how you are raising her now.

Dustin:

Well, I think about it every time I do something with her. How I work with her today will impact her future. I try to set things up with her like I do with young horses. I set it up so she learns and becomes confidant in herself and her abilities so that she can be a confidant young lady in the future. To me, with horses and humans it's no different. When I work with young horses, I think about what they're going to be in five,  ten, fifteen years. Who they may be under. What they may be doing if they are show horses or if they're going somewhere else. I've got an agenda for 'em. I try to give them all the confidence I can so that they are prepared for what life throws them in the future.

Paul:

Exactly. What you just said about not working on horses for today, but working on them for five, ten years from now, I believe is a really important point for leaders to think about. And, I've never heard anyone talk about it sincerely, the way you just did. It's not about managing for today's goals. It's about developing a team, developing your employees, your colleagues, and your peers for success tomorrow and beyond. It's focusing on what that future holds for each unique human being. There's a lot of effort now in professional development at work, so that you're always learning, you're always developing your future self. As leaders, we want to say, "I'm providing this professional development for my employees or my organization, so that they can be better than they are today, and it's not just about being better at their job, but better as human beings who might go on to do some world-changing things in the next five to ten years." That's how we should be thinking about professional development as opposed to, "I just sent them to be a better bean counter so they can come back and count beans even faster." As the business and nonprofit management guru Peter Drucker said, "The only way to predict the future is to create it." Create it for yourself. Create it for others. Don't wait for it to happen by chance.

Dustin:

I'm always working on my personal development, always asking myself, "How can I be better?" I want to be a better teacher. I want to be a better horseman. I want to be a better father. I want to be a better husband. I'm constantly working at that, because, to me, those are things that are important in life. I want to be successful. I see my brother-in-law John do that with his employees, and I have the utmost respect for him, because not only does he challenge them in their professional development, but there's also a little of that personal development he helps them with. They actually personally develop themselves as well as professionally. And over time, they become better employees, and they move themselves up the ranks. And I think a lot more leaders would be better if they did that for their team, challenging their employees to become better personally as well as professionally. Because, really, what I'm asking my clients to do when I have their horse they brought me is help the horse develop the professional side of themselves, if you will. Now, I'm also asking the owners to personally develop themselves and learn the stuff that their professionally-developed horse has learned so that they can be a better team and develop together. And that's something someone should probably take a good hard look at in life and could probably run a long way with.

Paul:
You're absolutely right. Your brother-in-law is addressing it correctly because who you are personally is who you bring to work professionally, to your job.

Often, when we first meet someone we tend to ask, "What do you do?" This makes me crazy, especially today when we have all kinds of different people doing all kinds of different things. What kind of question is that? As though it's some defining moment. And if your answer isn't what someone else expects or thinks is important, then they move on to somebody else. So if what you do comes from who you are, then that person is walking away because he or she didn't respect what you do, so they are really signaling, "I don't respect who you *are*." That's what you're talking about. For instance, when you see a show horse, that show horse isn't just a show horse. It's a horse that has a certain kind of personality and set of gifts. It just happens to also be a show horse, but the show horse duties aren't what defines it. So wouldn't it be an awesome world if when someone approached you they said, "Hi Dustin, *who* are you?" as opposed to, "Hi Dustin, *what* do you do?"

Dustin:
That would be refreshing.

Paul:
The other question often tied to "what do you do?" is "where do you live?" And people decide in that moment, based on what you do and where you live, if you are of enough importance to them to spend time talking with further. And I think that's so messed up, right? Because who the hell cares where you live or what you do? It's who you *are* that matters. And, one step further, we talk about redefining or restructuring culture and how culture is so important in a business because you spend so much time with these people every day, all day, all week. Culture is really important, so that makes the answer to who you are even more relevant to what you can do. We don't ask, "Who are you *really*?" I mean, maybe you do if you're best friends or after you've had a few too many glasses of wine, but we don't ask people who they are as often as we should. And yet, that's exactly what drives what they do. It should drive it, if they're present, if they're authentic, if they're open and centered in themselves. These are all the things that we've talked about that should matter.

Dustin:

I agree. And it's interesting to me because I really don't give a rat's ass about titles in life. They don't mean nothing to me because, as far as I'm concerned, the CEO puts his pants on the same way as a janitor puts his pants on. So it doesn't define anything different to me. I give both of them the same amount of respect and that's the way I was raised. That goes back to those ethics of what it means to be a cowboy to me, but I've always tried to, when the situation allows, not write anyone off within the first two seconds of meeting them regardless who they are, what they do, or where they live. If you can avoid those questions and get them to talk about themselves, usually the conversation gets deeper and there becomes an understanding, almost a relationship built pretty quickly between two people because you have stripped it down and become equally vulnerable. And it doesn't mean a damn thing if you live in Beverly Hills, Chino Hills, or you live out on bean hill. Does it really matter? We all come from the same place. Don't really matter to me. Doesn't matter what you do or how much money you got. None of that really means anything to me. It's about what you believe and what you value. What are your thoughts? What are your opinions? What are you passionate about? I mean, that'd be a really good one to ask somebody you meet for the first time, "What are your passions in life?" Well, that'd blow some people's socks off, wouldn't it?

Paul:

You say passion, and actually I have asked that question, but with a slightly different word. I ask them what "drives" them. And those drivers usually come from who you are and what you believe in. When I'm interviewing candidates for a job, there are many questions you can't legally ask, but there are two questions I always ask that give me deep insight as to who they are and what their potential is. The first one is, "Tell me about a moment in your career that was the most satisfying to you, and why?" Because that gets at the heart of passion and what they really feel is important. And then I ask them, "Tell me about a situation that was unfair in your career." That also gets at the heart of what they value. And that "unfair" question, in particular, has been a game-changer and an eye-opener for me because unfair is different than what makes you mad. Unfair equals unjust. Their answer allows me into their deepest beliefs that may even be unconscious to them. When they answer this "unfair" question and I think, "Hmm, that was a loaded answer," this little red flag appears. I've ignored that red flag a couple of times because I was desperate to hire someone, and damn it, if that didn't bite me because that "unfair" answer actually wound up being the reason I needed to fire that person for something in the future.

So what you're asking is how do you get to the heart of people? And, to your point, if when asked the question about their passion or their drive they look at you like a deer in the headlights or respond by asking, "What do you mean drive, passion? I just do what I do. I know what I know. I believe what I believe," then that also tells you a lot about them, doesn't it?

Dustin:
Oh, it does. I mean those two questions tell me a lot. If a person is gonna get pretty particular, if they're going to

say the most satisfying thing to them is making money, then that tells me, again, back to my point, you're skimming the surface of the pond of life my friend; there's not much to you. But if the most satisfying thing to you is knowing at the end of the week that you have done your duties or have fulfilled your passions, and you go home and get to spend time with your family, and you're extremely happy about that, and can provide for your family and that's what's most satisfying for you, then that's meaningful. That tells me you've got meaning and morals and reasons why you're doing what you're doing. And I bet you could poll two hundred people and one hundred fifty of them would have very shallow answers to these questions about their life. It'd be pretty interesting to test that.

Paul:

Funny you say that, because that just reminded me of a good friend and colleague of mine, Lee Wochner, whose classic question at the end of a candidate's interview is, "So, tell me what's the right way to fix a hamburger?" It's a weird question, right? But the reason he asks it is because he wants to know if they have ever thought about it. And if people hadn't even thought about that, then you know that they probably don't think critically about other things in their life if they're not even thinking about how to build the perfect hamburger. So that's an "aha" moment for him. And if people can't answer it in a very authentic way, then he

doesn't want them because they aren't critical or creative thinkers.

Dustin:

That's clever. That's someone who is truly looking for somebody who's going to be an asset to him. A lot of people would be like, that's not cool, because what if I didn't get the right answer to the hamburger he likes. He didn't ask you to fix his hamburger. He asked you to fix your hamburger.

Paul:

Exactly. Yes, it shows critical and creative thinking. These people are aware, have a thought, have a process, are thinking about life and the world, and aren't just putting their life on automatic pilot. For instance, when people default to, "I'm a certain religion," or "I'm a certain political party," or "I'm a certain whatever, and that's how I identify." And, again, that goes back to *what* you are, not *who* you are. So if you're a Democrat, that's what you are, but it's not who you are necessarily. I mean it could be for some, but it's not necessarily so for everyone.

Dustin:

For sure. I think people get so hung up on titles, like a job title, or they're Catholic or they're Republican or they're Mormon, but that doesn't define who they are. Those are just, to me, those are just taglines or a heading of something in life. You know, that'd be like me walking up to a horse and saying, "She's a Democrat, huh? I don't like that." That don't mean a damn to me.

Paul:
Also to your point, it signals to the other person that I know exactly the type of horse or person they are since every Democrat is the same. But that simply is not the case. And, how narrow-minded would that be? But we all want that easy understanding of who people are based on their identity, title, or life's tagline, as you put it.

Dustin:
Right.

Paul:
People consciously or unconsciously judge each other, and yet how many times have you walked up to a Democrat or a Republican or a Mormon or a Catholic and they say something to you that didn't sound very Mormon or that didn't sound very Republican? Because there's a lot of grey. People aren't just this or that. It's extremely complicated.

Dustin:
It's like we used to say in Oklahoma all the time, "How do you keep a Baptist from drinking all your beer? Take another Baptist with you." That's the only way you can keep 'em honest, you know? It's just one of those deals, so it doesn't mean anything. You just go with it and it's just life. You are who you are; it doesn't matter. Reminds me of the saying, "I am who I am." If you like me, great, if you don't, it's kinda your problem. That's your choice not to like me. If you didn't get to know me, that's really not my problem.

I'm not going to change who I am for you. That's how

I try and look at all of my horses. They have personalities. They are who they are. I have this one horse. He's real touchy, and that's fine by me. No one else wants to ride him. No one wants anything to do with him, but I love that horse to death and I'll do right by him until he dies, and I'm not asking him to change if that's how he has to live his life. I will help him in every way I possibly can to get through that, and I will ride him as much as I possibly can, and we will stay together. I'm not going to sell him because he's that way. You know, other people tell me to sell him, but that's not a good solution. No, he's got something to teach me, and I can learn from him. I'm gonna hang in there and be his partner as he will be mine and we'll get all the way through it, whatever life throws at us. I know people that throw them away for a lot less and it's like, man, where's the commitment of hanging onto something to see it through to its potential?

Paul:

Absolutely. It's interesting because people have developed their personality and who they are by the age of seven. And it's futile for us to try to undo that because we're not going to undo it. And, yet, we spend so much time trying to fight that battle of undoing a personality as opposed to finding those places where we have commonality or where our passions are the same and starting from that place and then seeing how far we can go with someone's potential. But so many of us want to change the other person, tell the other person why their idea is wrong, or their philosophy is wrong, or their approach to life is wrong. Well, what are those things that you both agree on and what if you started the conversation there? Then, if you have a disagreement, you can lean on the trust you already started building in the relationship that will allow you to have the harder conversations, as opposed to going for the jugular the minute there is a difference of opinion.

Dustin:
Exactly.

Paul:
We sound so smart.

Dustin:
Right? Smart or just make each other think that. One of the two. I haven't figured it out yet.

Paul:
I don't know what you got in your cup but I got a shot of gin here...no, I'm kidding.

Dustin:
I'm not.

Paul:
Well, they do say the closer you get to the bottom of a bottle, the smarter you get.

Dustin:
I guess. I oughta be damn smart by now. Let me tell you.

Paul:
This reminds me of a billboard that I actually saw while I was driving in Minneapolis one day. It was a whiskey

advertisement, and it claimed, "Makes Your Band Sound Better." So there it is.

Dustin:
There is truth to that.

Connecting the Dots

There is no doubt that what you do today will affect your tomorrow. It seems simple, yet it is so profound. What if you were strategic and intentionally planned on having what you do today produce an effect on your tomorrow ten years from now? That is what we call a paradigm shift. And it must come from within you.

Your profession does not define you, who you *are* does. Who you are impacts what you do, how you do it, and why you do it. Therefore, you must understand what drives you. This passion will guide you to your purpose. That purpose will pull you. However, none of this will matter unless you tap into your potential. That potential will push you. Your potential is the most powerful arrow in your quiver.

Potential yields possibility. Possibility yields endless solutions. Endless solutions force us into the world of grey.

Despite our survivalist beginnings, we have figuratively become a bit like couch potatoes when it comes to really challenging situations that require a thoughtful response. When we rely on how we self-identify, we run the risk of allowing our critical thinking to get stuck on autopilot. For instance, if we affiliate with a certain political or religious group, we tend to respond to an extremely complex question with a definitive black-and-white answer based on our affiliation instead of independently scrutinizing it through the lens of grey.

Potential opens us to possibility which eventually makes us confront the grey. How we handle the grey is ultimately what defines us, and how others will remember us.

Cowboy-Conductor Challenge

To take inventory of your current team's potential or determine a job applicant's future growth in your organization, find out what they score on our Three Cs Test™. Are they Curious? Are they Creative? Are they Committed?

Curious people try to fix the unfixable, answer the unanswerable.

⇒ To test for this, present the individual with a problem you are trying to solve that matches their current or future job expectations. If it is an accounting position, give them a financial example. If it is an architectural position, give them a form and function example. The problem you use could be a real one that you have yet to solve, or one that you fabricate but present as real.

⇒ Start off with a question such as, "I have been trying to figure this out all week. There doesn't seem to be a solution. I've tried over and over to solve it. I've asked others to help me solve it. What do you think about it?"

⇒ Watch for their immediate reaction. If it is unbounded excitement to figure it out, then you have the right person for the team. If it is tentative, or overwhelmed, then you have the wrong artist for the masterpiece you want to create.

If they pass the Curious test, you need to find out if they are Creative enough to solve for the problem you posed earlier.

⇒ Come up with a problem that could have a number of solutions or requires creative mastery to even begin to solve. Their answer does not have to actually solve the problem. What you are determining is how they get to the answer they give you.

⇒ Have them talk through their solution with you. This will give you an excellent idea of their thought process.

⇒ Add some of your own ideas or questions to see if they lean toward being a team player or prefer sole domination.

⇒ Remember, it is more important to understand their process than have them come up with a plausible solution. To paraphrase Ralph Waldo Emerson, "It's about the journey, not the destination."

If they have now passed both the Curious and Creative sections of our Three Cs Test™, you need to determine if they are Committed. It is fantastic to have curious and creative team members, but if they are not committed to following through, their impact will be severely blunted.

⇒ While this may not be time-efficient, the best way to test for commitment is to observe them in action. Your assigned problem from above might be too unwieldy to test, so you may have to create a smaller problem to solve, or you can take a section of the problem to gauge commitment.

⇒ If it is a current employee, give them the task and a timeline to complete it. If it is a job applicant, make finishing the task within your timeline the final part of the job interview process.

⇒ In either case, you will find out whether they could or could not deliver on it. Warning: do not let their creative excuses for not being able to complete the task on time allow them a pass. If you set a reasonable and attainable goal, they should be able to complete it. If they fail, they are signaling that they cannot do it or do not care enough. Neither is acceptable.

It all comes down to The Three Cs. People who have higher levels of curiosity, creativity, and commitment are far more likely to meet or exceed their natural potential. These are the team members and candidates who will deliver on their potential to positively impact your organization.

ON PERSPECTIVE

Saddling Up

Perspective is the way in which you view something. It is also an art technique that changes the distance or depth of an object, creating an illusion. Mirrors can create illusions. Take for instance the safety message on your car's side-view mirror, "Objects in the mirror may be closer than they appear." So, what do you need to do? You need to look over your shoulder to get another angle, another perspective - the perspective of reality. If you take at face value the things you perceive, without questioning or having a second look from another angle, you may be endangering yourself, those in your care, or your organization's future. This is our perspective on perspective.

Conversation

Dustin:

You spoke about focusing on developing leaders. So when you go into a business or organization that hires you to help them make their teams stronger, and they need to make changes in developing the team to make them stronger, but really it's the leader that needs to make a change, how do you direct that in ways that can help that leader make the change in order to help the development of the team he or she leads?

Paul:

That's the million-dollar question! When I go into an organization, I do a holistic organizational assessment which begins by looking at the data such as their financials, governing documents, bylaws, employee handbook, things that will give me facts and tell me the story of where they've been and where there are now. So that's the black-and-white piece of it. The grey piece of it is talking to all the key leaders and stakeholders. I listen for themes as I did when I was a conductor. Perhaps I'm hearing a common theme of micromanagement, or frustration, or lack of clarity. Then I can go back and have a conversation with that leader and say, "Here are some common themes I heard." I keep all of the conversations completely confidential, not attributing any of the themes to any one person. These themes usually tie back to the data. For instance, if there is frustration or low morale, that might also show in the financials, which may be flat or declining over a long period. Sometimes the governing documents, such as the employee handbook, will be written punitively, and that will be affecting morale. So it's really about tying the data and themes together, then delivering them in an objective way. I help them understand that it's not just about their leadership, it's about the success or failure of their team or their company. So if they care about that, there are ways I can help them turn it around. But some don't see the urgency or want to put the time or money into fixing the problem. They must make the choice. It's not for me to decide. As you very well know the old saying, "You can lead a horse to water...."

We talked about consultants having a bad reputation, but I think that the best consultants are there to present options that are based in data. They are non-emotional and their objective is to help further the success of the organization. Then the onus is on the client to make the best decision given the recommendations.

I use this same objective, goal-oriented approach when leading intense negotiations where each side might be starting in completely opposite corners. In those cases, it's best to ask both sides, "What is the common goal?" And many times, the common goal is not emotional. So if the common goal is to provide enough work to the union employees for example, yet they want to impose restrictive rules in the contract, the employer may go out of business and then those union employees will be out of work. In this case, I might say to the union employees, "It's clear our common goal is to gainfully employ you at this company in a way that is successfully sustainable. So, what can we do to get there?" And it's the same thing with the leader. You know, it's really about taking the emotion and the personal out of it, and talking about the common goals of that team or that business. It's keeping all these things in perspective.

Dustin:

That's fascinating to me to talk about the themes. For example, when someone brings me a problem horse, the owner will tell me what the problems are, and then I work with the horse and the horse shows me what the real problems are.

So I basically have these two that disagree, the horse and the human. Then I try to find the common ground so that both of them can work together. And then usually I have to go back in and I have to take the human emotion out of it so that I can get them both on the same page. So in a lot of ways, it's very similar how both of us work. It's really fascinating to me.

Paul:

What's interesting about what you just said is often my first point of contact is with whoever's hiring me. It usually is the CEO or the owner of the company, a decision-maker. And I'll go in and I'll ask, "So what's the problem?" And like your example, they'll say, "Well, this is the problem, and this is what needs to be done." But instead of taking their point of view as fact, I'll suggest an organizational assessment where we can review the governing documents and talk to the key stakeholders. And they'll usually say, "We don't need to talk to everybody, I already know the problem. Just come in here and fix it." Interestingly enough, if I just listened to that leader and said to myself, "OK, well, that's the problem, and I need to go work with his or her employees and get to the heart of this," I would already be off on the wrong foot because I've made assumptions based on what I had heard from only one source. And I would say one hundred percent of the time, when I've talked to the owner or the person who hired me who said definitively, "This is what's going on," once I get into the one-on-one employee interviews, it's not at all the problem that I heard from the owner. There are all these other issues that wind up being the foundation of what's really causing the problems. So I ask myself, "What are the drivers causing those issues?" So for sure, like you said, you have to get the horse's side of it.

Dustin:

It's very much the same when I have someone who wants to bring their horse in. I'll suggest an evaluation. They'll tell me everything that's going on, and I say, "Great, here's what it's going to cost; this is what we need to do." They agree that it sounds good. Then they show up and they have to tell me everything they told me on the phone all over again before they ever get the horse out of the trailer. And by the time they get their horse from the trailer to the ground and enter the arena, the horse has already spoken, and I think, "Wow, there's a huge disagreement going on right here to begin with." Like you're saying, I can't just work off the owner's story. You learn through time, through experience, that a lot of different things people are telling you, what they're saying, you have to remind yourself, "OK, I kinda know where that's at." It's using those little tools you have, but you're never quick to prejudge because anytime you do, something new is going to rear its ugly head, and you're gonna think, "Didn't see that one coming!" So I watch them work together, and then I evaluate. It's the same thing. It all lays out there in front of you if you allow it.

Paul:

What you're saying is every time you prejudge it shuts down a piece of your being open to what could be happening and diminishes your ability to actually be successful in fixing whatever that core problem is. It can alter your perspective. So if the owner brought the horse to you and said, "Here are the three things that need fixing," and you replied, "Great, let's get at them, let's start fixing those," just assuming those were the three things that were wrong with them, you could be spending all this time doing more damage because you didn't leave yourself open to other possibilities. So the more you prejudge, the more you have it all prefigured out, which is why I don't trust anyone who's got everything figured out. You're shutting down possibilities and answers and solutions that you may not even know you're supposed to be exploring.

Dustin:

Here's a good example of that. I had a lady bring me a horse. It was her daughter's paint horse. She told me just before they were getting ready to go to the world show, the horse was kicking out at her leg any time she asked for the lope. She put the spur on it and the horse would kick out. So they brought it to the professional trainer, and the professional trainer worked on it, and by the time the professional trainer got done, the horse had bucked everybody off, and was rearing up and everything else. And so they called me and said you need to cowboy through it and just ride the buck out of this horse so the horse learns to take the spur. So I told Aimee, "Well I guess they just want to make a bronc ride." So I go over there and fiddle around for a little bit. And I said, "Just give me ten days with this horse. That's all I ask. Just ten days. Let me take it home, work with it and we'll have things fixed up." They say, "Oh, we can't do that." Now I assume, of course, the professional trainer didn't want to lose any money or whatever else. I said, "Look, you're still gonna make money off the top of me, because you're paying him way the hell more than I'm charging so it'll be fine. Just let me have the horse for ten days." So I brought the horse home, never wore a spur, gave the horse a new job, and in ten days they came over and got ready to ride. And the girl straps her spurs on and I said, "Just take them off. You're not going to need them." And she says, "But this horse has had to have spurs from day one." And I said, "I'll bet you. I'll bet you double or nothing what my expenses are, what I'm going to charge you, that you will not need those, and you can do your entire pattern without a spur on either foot." Fine. Sure enough, she got on there, the horse never kicked out. Never. She did the entire pattern perfectly.

Well, shoot, that was great! But they didn't pay me double, of course.

Paul:
I was gonna ask.

Dustin:

No, of course not. They didn't pay me double because they didn't believe it. So what do they do? They go back to the world show and start warming this horse up and using spurs again. The professional trainer calls me from the world show. The night before the performance, the horse started kicking out again. I asked him, "You put spurs on, didn't you?" And he replied, "Well, I ride everything that way." I said, "I understand that, but I told you that horse is sick and tired of being kicked with a spur. You would get that way, too. This is what you need to do, don't let her ride in a pair of spurs for the show tomorrow. I guarantee you she'll be fine." So what do they do? They did it. I watched it on the show. She didn't wear her spurs. She won the youth world show. Come home, lady said, "What did you do with our horse?" I said, "All I did is chase cows around for ten days in the pasture. So the horse *wanted* to go to the lope, and didn't want to kick out at my foot. That's all I did. I just went and rode around and chased cows." It was great for me. Hell, I had more fun doing that than I did riding anything else. But again, I started off keeping an open mind to the problem. The horse just needed to find a new way, a new reason to want to take those leads. And, again, if you prejudge it, you're going to lose it, and you've got to be open to whatever can happen.

Paul:

And another layer is matching that horse's desire with a change in behavior. It's the same thing with people. If you just discipline them or manage them in a way that they don't want to be managed and you're not open and sensitive to what you actually need to be providing them to succeed, they will continue to be ornery. What's interesting is that in a case where a manager is having trouble with an employee, really what that employee might be is bored or agitated by doing the same job. And the manager, because they see the agitation or boredom, thinks, "Well, I'm certainly not going to give that person more responsibility." But your example shows that's actually the opposite approach they should take. It's kind of like the horse spurs. If you gave that person more responsibility, and they become engaged more in their job, they're going to not have the same boredom and low performance that they had before. And yet, we don't. We believe if we just yell at them more or discipline them more with a spur in their side that'll fix the situation.

Dustin:
Right.

Paul:
Sometimes it's letting them free, letting them roam, letting them be, empowering them to do what they actually want to do, and giving them more work as opposed to less.

Dustin:
Again, it's interesting. If you do it right once, both flourish. You've got to be open-minded to that stuff and have the right perspective. It's the same with a horse. I had a horse owner send me what was supposed to be a western pleasure horse and he just was not happy doing his job. I brought him over here. He just happened to like the cows over the fence. So I tried it one day and I mean he was a roping fool. So what happened? We sold him for a rope

horse, and doubled the girl's money and she went and bought a different horse. And I'm like, no harm, no foul. You made twice what you paid for him and you went and bought a horse that did the job you wanted to do, and everyone's happy. There's a win-win all the way around.

Paul:
Exactly.

Dustin:
When you're setting things up like that in life, how can you complain? I'm the type of person that the glass isn't half full. It isn't half empty. I just look at it and say it needs to be refilled. What difference does it make? Doesn't matter if it's half empty or half full - top it off and let's go.

Paul:
That's funny. So I'm a glass overflowing person, and you know how fun that is!

Dustin:
Yeah, right? We make a great pair, don't we?

Paul:
I swim around in the beauty of an overflowing glass.

Dustin:
Fun!

Paul:
So, back at the ranch, so to speak, we've talked about assessing an organization, assessing employees. When

assessing a troubled horse, what are those specific things you look for? I told you what I look for. Actually, I didn't tell you exactly what I look for, so let's dig deeper here for both of us. When you assess a troubled horse, what are those things you're considering? What are those things that you're looking for, sensing, feeling? Whatever the problems are, there must be similar key things that you are assessing.

Dustin:
Well, it can be really subtle because there can be so many different problems you are trying to address.

Paul:
Let me go first then to give you an idea of what I'm asking.

Dustin:
Okay.

Paul:
When I go in and talk to people, the questions I'm asking them will be specific to whatever the problem is that we're trying to solve. But what I'm listening for, what I'm assessing, is are they being honest with me? Are they saying one thing, but really thinking something else? What does their body language tell me? Are they telling me something that needs to be improved because it's going to be better for them? Or is it actually better for the company? What are their motives? I sort that out. I'm going through an organizational assessment right now and I've talked to thirteen people this past week and there are one or two of them who are really thinking about

what's in it for them and not what's best for the company. And yet, a handful of them really said, "Wow, if we could change this, it would be so awesome for everybody, so awesome for the company, and then we'd have so much more fun and be so much more successful!" I listen to those troubled people, those troubled horses, in different ways and come to different conclusions based on what they tell me and what the data says.

Dustin:

It is a lot the same way for me. That's why I like to do assessments and evaluations for horses, especially when someone calls me and they got a problem horse. I really try and get them here with their horse to evaluate it, because it paints the whole picture for me. To see them interact with their horse and how they are. I watch, like you, their body language. I listen to their speech. They'll call me on the phone and they're cool and they're collected, and they got this nice little canned speech that they probably wrote up or who knows? They've thought about this long and hard before they called me. When I start swinging questions at them, it trips them up every time. Usually, I'll talk to them for five minutes because they'll get out and they'll be so nervous and just jumping around and I think, "You need to calm down because your horse and my horses are bouncing off the stalls because they're wondering what is wrong with that lady or that guy?!" Jiminy Christmas! And, so, they'll talk a little bit and once they kind of get that off their chest, they'll level off just a little bit, then they start to anticipate what's going to happen when they crack the trailer door open. And I just reassure them, "Hey, I'm right here. You have nothing to worry about."

If we're taking the horse to the round pen, I'll watch how they're both reacting, how the horse is reacting, and how they are reacting to each other, to their surroundings. Usually, I'll tell them, "Why don't you turn the horse loose for a minute." Most of them act like they are flying a kite. They get here. They're worked up. The horse then gets worked up. The horse is zinging around. So I just say, "Turn him loose, let him move for a few minutes." I'll stand right there next to the round pen while that horse is running laps and the owners will be standing ten feet off to the other side out by their trailer. And I think, "Where in the hell do you think you're going? Your horse is in here. There's no need to be out there unless he's going to jump the fence." And that tells me that they're pretty closed off about this deal. They assume it's definitely the horse, it's not them. And, so then, you'll watch the owner, they walk up here and they have their arms crossed and they say, "Well, there ain't nothing you're gonna fix." And I listen to them talk, and they say, "You know, when I go ride this horse, this is how he acts or when I go to the barn to get him out of his stall, he does this." What I hear is, "This is what he does to me." The way they word stuff tells me a lot about what their thought process is. They think it's the horse doing it to them intentionally, which is never the case. The horse is reacting to them. But they tell you a whole lot without saying a whole lot, just in the way they speak about their horse.

Then I ask them to go in and do something with their horse. I'll watch their body language and how they move. And then, usually, I say, "Well, let me see him for a second." And I'll take the halter or lead rope, and let them walk out of the round pen and I'll stand there and talk for another five minutes. And I'm going to do a couple of things and set a few little ground rules real quick. Usually, it isn't very long and that horse will be standing there. And the owner is still just as worked up as they were when they were in there themselves. And they say, "Why is he just standing there with you? He doesn't do that with me." So I quietly suggest, "Maybe you need to take a look in the mirror real quick and ask yourself the question you just asked me. If he'll stand here with me, why won't he stand here with you?" And then there's other cases where I'll walk in there and the horse is a handful. And I'm like, OK, you've gotten away with this long enough, and, yeah, there are some deep-seated issues in you that the humans taught you that we need to get straightened out. And, so I just kinda listen to what the horse has to tell me. Then I try and see what they say. The owners will tell me, "I love this horse to death. You know, I've raised him since he was a baby, and once I weaned him from his mommy, I did this, this, and this." So then I let them know that they projected the mother role on the horse and catered to him. So I just kinda have to keep dissecting it to see where we're at, like you do. And see if they're looking for a partnership with that horse.

I'll have some clients say, "I want to spend the rest of my life with the horse. I just want to figure out how to get through this to where we can get along and be on the same page, and we can get through this together." And then there's others who say, "I just need you to fix this so I can go ride and he's gonna listen to me." And it's like, OK, so we're doing this for you, not for the horse. That pretty much tells me what's what. And I've had some of those cases come in here and they'll say, "This is what you need to do." And I say, "Well, then I'm not your guy. I hate to tell you that, but I appreciate your time." Usually about that quick, they're backstepping really fast, and ask, "Well, why?" And I tell them, "Because you're not taking into consideration anything the horse has been offering you." I kinda rock them back a little bit and say, "Now think about this...." I'll put it back on them. And some of them, they'll say, "I never thought of it that way. I want to try this. I want to figure it out."

You just got to dig a little bit to figure it out what they truly want from inside of them, for them and for that horse. So it's a lot the same thing. I'm sensing body language. I'm listening to how people speak. I'm listening to what their intentions are, what they want down the road, and how they want to present things to me, to their horse. In a lot of ways, how they present things to me explains to me and shows me how they're presenting things to their horse.

Paul:

And they're usually dismissive of your idea to just bring their horse to you and have it spend time with you, right? They say, "I already told you what the problem is. Don't waste my money by keeping him here for five days doing your soft stuff. You're huggy, feely stuff." I have the same issue with my clients. When going into troubled companies who have hit a plateau, the first thing they ask me is, "How do we fix the financials? How can we improve net income? I want to grow the business. I want to increase the bottom line." So I respond, "Well, what's happening with your employees? What's your organizational structure? How do you operate day to day?" They usually push back with, "That's not important. All I need you to do is fix the financial situation."

And I respond the same way you do to your horse owners. I say, "Well, I need to look at the whole of it. I need to observe what's happening. How you're managing the company. How the structure works. What is the decision-making matrix? How do your employees feel about this or that? Are things being run efficiently and effectively?" All those things affect the bottom line, which is the net income they want  improved. And just like with you, they have to examine all these other things which will affect the bottom line. You can't just go in and start fixing XYZ until you really understand the whole picture of what's going on. And, it's the same frustration that I have with people who want to hire me to fix just one thing. I think that's the biggest takeaway, which is you have to approach business, people, and horses in a holistic way. You can't fix one thing without it affecting another. You have to make sure that the entire body works. With an orchestra, if you give the wrong signal to just one musician, it can have a ripple effect throughout the entire orchestra. If you're having a pain in your chest, maybe that might be coming from your head or it might be coming from your foot. You can't just look at that one little area. You have to take a holistic approach to the problems which will get you to the right solutions.

Dustin:

Very much so. I know I've heard it many times, "My horse does this, what do I do?" And I say, "Well, it depends." And they bite back, "What do you mean, it depends?" My mentor Ray is the king of asking, "Well, what happened before what happened happened? That's how we can fix it." For me, I'm dealing with a living, breathing, decision-making animal.

Paul:

Exactly.

Dustin:

They get sick, they get well, they get hot, they get cold, they get tired, they get energetic. You gotta take all that into consideration, and people don't. They expect them to work like a machine, and I don't want my horses to be machines. Like I said before, if I wanted a machine, I'd go be a damn farmer, and there's nothing wrong with farming. We're all brethren, whether you're farming or you're cowboying. We've got to understand we're dealing with the same thing, but people don't look at it that way. Especially the power games where the humans put themselves above horses. In my world, the horse is way above the human.

Paul:

Because?

Dustin:

Well, the horse just deserves more than the human can offer. The horse is up here and the human is down there. Humans are so busy trying to drag that horse down to their level instead of raising themselves to the level of the horse. Kind of like we were talking about earlier, your professional side and your personal side, your employers trying to drag you one way and your personal instincts pulling the other direction. Well, why not develop both sides to meet in the middle? If the horse can operate from way up there, why can't you learn to raise yourself to operate where that horse is or at least meet them in the middle?

Paul:
And I'd imagine also, given our conversations that the horse is on a higher plane because they don't have all the baggage that we have.

Dustin:
Right.

Paul:
So if the horse is more authentically thinking and acting and behaving, why should we start with our preconceived notions as a human? We should start with the natural state of what a horse brings and what a horse needs. We need to be open to all perspectives.

Dustin:
The horse remembers what you did yesterday but he starts each day anew just trying to survive so he can see tomorrow. And the human, they come in today thinking about what happened yesterday and how they're gonna reconcile it today. This idea that he did this to me yesterday so this is what I'm going to do to inflict

something on him today. The horse doesn't think about why he bucked you off yesterday or if you're gonna come to the barn today or if you're gonna put some God-awful medieval rig on him and try and ride him again. He just thinks, "That's in the past man, let's move on. Let's move forward." Well, why can't the human do that? It is what it is. Chalk it up as lesson learned and move on. Start your day the same way he did. I got up this morning and saw the sun come up while feeding the greatest animals on Earth. How is that not the best way to start your day! I'm not saying that there aren't other great ways. But for me, watching the sun come up on a new day, feeding your best friends, I mean, how does life get any better than that?

Paul:

That idea goes back to focusing on what our drivers are. The horse may not be thinking about that, because the horse doesn't think that way. But, yet, we are imposing our own thoughts and beliefs on that horse, just like we do on people. We all have different drivers and motives so, when we communicate, we have to keep that in mind. We can't automatically assume what the message is and then react to it without clarification. That's how discussions and conflicts escalate. It's what I call the Assumption Xceleration Theory™ - AssX for short.

Dustin:

Exactly

Paul:

We tend to assume they were trying to piss us off and so we're going to get back at them even though they just said something out of turn or weren't even thinking about it. How we react should depend on the other person's intention. We have to be flexible. We shouldn't just AssX it.

As we discussed before, so many people want to have the solution in black and white. The unknown is what makes life fun, right? The grey. If you've got everything figured out, then you already know what's going to happen the rest of your life. How boring is that?

Dustin:

A good friend told me the other day, "You've never seen a U-Haul following a hearse." You can't take a damn thing with you when you go. So why not live every day and enjoy the moments that you have with what you have instead of trying to acquire more. If you can't find happiness in what you have, you're never going to find it.

Some of the happiest people I know or ever met in my life probably have the least number of things, and they truly are the happiest people. Look at children. They have absolutely no worries because they're taken care of. They have no real wants except for when they learn that they can want things and they can receive things, but otherwise, as long as they're fed, that's pretty much all they really need in life, and they're happy.

Paul:

So wouldn't it be awesome if we could keep the perspective that as long as we are fed and can breathe and have water, the basic things that keep us alive as humans, then everything else would be a bonus?

Dustin:

Exactly, wouldn't that make life so much better?

Paul:

So it's all how you approach life. Let's strive for being like those who say, "I'm just happy that I'm alive this morning, and if anything else good happens to me, that's a bonus today," as opposed to, "I need five great things to happen to me today for me to be satisfied by the time I go to bed tonight." Completely different approaches.

Dustin:

They are. We've got some friends that do that and it just cracks me up every time I turn around. They say, "Have you seen what so-and-so is doing on Facebook or Instagram?" Oh my God, the next thing is they went and bought a newer vehicle or they bought a bigger house. And I think, "You guys are in debt farther than you could ever pay off in your life. Are you happy?" If you have to think about that for even a split second, you're not. Life is just that simple, and what's it going to take? You need a million dollars, and will that make you happy? Well, that would pay off all my debt, but then I'd be broke again. So you're saying you need two million to make you happy? If so, then you're a greedy son of a bitch. If I give you a dollar, you should be happy. It's a dollar you didn't have before we started this conversation. That's just the way I look at it, but sometimes I'm a little too simple I think.

Paul:

No, you're absolutely right. It's almost as if they have an illness and they won't address the fundamental reasons for the illness and all they do is drink alcohol to make themselves feel better. It only lasts for a little bit until that alcohol wears off and then they need more alcohol. But, if you actually address the illness, you can try to figure out what's at the heart of it by going back to the foundation that we talked about, whether its training or dealing with horses or people. If you take care of the foundation, then you won't need all the other bullshit that people pile on it.

Dustin:

True. Maybe I'm more thankful for the things I've had in my life and the doors that have opened for me in the path that I have taken, but I've been to the bottom of the barrel of life and even been below that layer of scum where things were just so bad that if I woke up the next morning, it was a hell of a good day for me. So whatever little things I can find that make me happy in life, I'm going to love them!

More people should be that way. Because I've been in high places and had great things happen, and have also had the whole rug jerked out from under me and it wasn't my fault. And I figured out how to rally back. It happened to me and I'm thankful that it happened because I learned so many great things from it.

Paul:

That resilience is in all of us.

It's the same resilience in that horse that's been beaten and beaten and beaten. It takes a long time to get down to the bottom of the barrel and below, and if we realize that it's our natural tendency to be resilient and strong, then trust that inner strength.

We must allow ourselves to self-heal, as opposed to saying, "Well, I'm below the bottom of the barrel and there's no way I can crawl back up again" or "There's no way to fix that problem person or that problem horse." We all have a natural tendency to rise up from that bottom should we choose to do it.

Dustin:

I agree with you, and people try and help you. I was never looking for a handout. I might've been looking for a hand up, but I was never looking for a handout on my way back up, and I wish more people would work at it that way and really try and be resilient. And I think that's why my passion for the horse is so strong, because I've seen him come from the other side, and make that turnaround, and it is a phenomenal thing to see.

Paul:

I think that is what probably drives your passion and gives you such a positive perspective. Every day you see those horses and all they want to do is be resilient and be great horses, and yet we drag them down. Constantly.

And with your work, you're always around this sort of natural resilience and positivity. Everything's the best. And I would bet it makes you so furious when you see that sunshine, that joy of life diminished, or that candle snuffed out knowing that it took a lot to snuff that candle out.

Dustin:

Oh yeah. It takes a lot. It's sad to see.

Connecting the Dots

Having perspective suggests that you have knowledge of and experience in whatever it is you are considering. That perspective should extinguish prejudice. Prejudice is the enemy of possibility. Possibility fuels passion. Passion drives desire. And desire is the key to break through change. So your perspective matters. But, more importantly, your educated, thoroughly-vetted perspective matters.

Our initial perspective overlaid with reality is what causes our disconnect. Therefore, you must adopt a *nothing is as it seems* approach to your view of the world. This will allow you to have the freedom to question what might be presented to you as the obvious. Questioning is not disbelieving; it is a strategy of verification. Questioning allows you to step back and not immediately assume you have it all figured out. The employee who is always temperamental may be suffering from a personal trauma at home that is playing out at work. The absolutely bored team member that tends to give the least amount of effort may not be lazy, they may be under-challenged at work. So instead of giving them less responsibility, you might need to give them much more which will greatly improve their performance and impact. As with horses, if we give humans the space to roam freely, that may generate greater satisfaction which might develop deeper loyalty. Yet we tend to assume the opposite, that they will take advantage of our generosity and produce negative results.

Sometimes, we do not have people or life all figured out. Those who say they do must lead an incredibly boring existence as they already profess to have figuratively read the last sentence of the book of life. For those of us who have not read the last page, remember that we can create our own ending if we so desire. We can write a tragic ending or a heroic one. We decide. We build our own barriers which means we can take them down, when, and if, we want.

Decide what is going to be your perspective on perspective.

Cowboy-Conductor Challenge

Perspective is derived from viewing something from different angles or viewpoints.

One simple and fun way you can build upon your perspective at team meetings is to take time to interpret a piece of abstract art. This could be a drawing, a painting, a sculpture or whatever you find that is intriguing. The more abstract, the more fun you will have. Project the work on a screen so that everyone can see it. Have each person, in silence, come up with what they think the piece is depicting. Then when everyone has their thoughts complete, ask each person to share what they think it is and how they came to that conclusion. There is no right or wrong answer. This will do two things. One, it will get everyone critically thinking. And, two, it will more closely bond those team members who have similar thoughts and reasonings.

A second way to expand your perspective, that requires no preparation and is easy to execute, is to invite a team member to secretly join in on a complex conversation of yours, assuming it is both legally and ethically possible. Do not let the other person, or persons with whom you are having the conversation, know your team member is listening. Also, make sure your team member does not suddenly participate. Proceed with the conversation as you normally would. Afterwards, meet with your team member and ask what they thought of the meeting, your position or strategy, how you delivered the information or answered the questions, and what they thought of the outcome. Lastly, ask if they would have done anything differently, and why. Make sure you are not defensive when they give you their perspective. Comparing notes with each other will be enlightening for you both, and serve as a lesson in strategy and approach, as well as perspective.

The more we train ourselves to observe things through a multi-angled, holistic lens, the more intuitive we will be in recognizing that, at first glance, things are often not what they seem.

ON EMOTIONAL INTELLIGENCE

Saddling Up

There are numerous articles and studies that suggest most CEOs were C students, including the book by Robert Kiyosaki titled, *Why "A" Students Work for "C" Students*. While their fellow students were ingesting all the academic information they could get to pass the class and focus on one specialty, these future CEOs were delighting in the world of possibility and purpose. As a matter of fact, Facebook's Mark Zuckerberg, Microsoft's Bill Gates, and Oprah Winfrey all dropped out of college to pursue their own paths as entrepreneurs. If not a college degree, what do extraordinary entrepreneurs rely upon for success? Part of the answer to this question may be found in emotional intelligence.

Conversation

Paul:

We talked about emotional intelligence the other day, which is about self-awareness. It's understanding who you are, how you're feeling, and how you show up to work or to your partner or to your friends. It's also about being able to self-regulate so that if you are angry because you just spilled your hot coffee on your lap on the way to work, you know you're going to regulate yourself so you're not going to take that out on everyone you come across in the next two hours. Another part of emotional intelligence is internal motivation where you have to desire it. You have to want it and own it. You can't be told to do it or told to love it. The fourth part of emotional intelligence is empathy, understanding where other people are coming from and meeting them where they are as opposed to hammering in your opinion. Lastly, it is having the social skills to be able to mix and mingle with all kinds of different people.

Conductors, and actually all performers, must possess emotional intelligence if they want to be successful. Because it doesn't matter how you feel that day, the show must go on! And as a conductor, you are the coach. You can't have a bad day. You can't let the outside world interfere with you inspiring others to be their best. You must be centered and empathetic, even when it seems virtually impossible.

I think back to that herd mentality where you have all

kinds of different horses: small, short, different coats, different classes, male, female; and yet, they all socialize with each other in the most ideal way. With them, I don't know if there's the emotional intelligence that I just mentioned, an awareness, regulation, motivation, or empathy. But, certainly, social skills seem to be very similar within the herd mentality.

Dustin:

There's a lot of social skill with it. I don't know if all of emotional intelligence with horses breaks down quite as far as you just mentioned.

Paul:

Perhaps there is a self-awareness?

Dustin:

There sure is self-awareness in the horses.

Paul:

I would say that one's internal motivation is that energy level you mentioned earlier, awareness and energy.

Dustin:

Yeah, because they're aware of the energy of the other horses. They are aware of you.

Paul:

And do they self-regulate? Do they have different levels of regulation?

Dustin:

Oh yeah. Take for instance, a horse pushing on another horse. They'll be grazing and one will walk up there, and they'll pin their ears and kick at each other. And a couple of seconds later, they both have their heads down and they're grazing again. The energy went up; the energy came right back down. They turn it up and turn it down. It isn't a big deal. They just do it in a way that is different than humans.

Paul:

Sure, but they even have the empathy, right? You mentioned earlier about how horses will circle a sick horse and stay with it as opposed to saying, "Oh too bad, man. Tough luck, see you later."

Dustin:

Yeah.

Paul:

It seems as though they have all five levels of emotional intelligence. And yet we treat them the way we do even though they are much more advanced than we are as a human race.

Dustin:

In a way I think they are.

Paul:

The exception being that horses aren't able to send themselves to the moon.

Dustin:

They actually may be smarter than us to be honest with you. A horse is a mirror of you and your energy level. They can sense what's going on with you and people just don't understand that. I show owners that exact point over and over again. They are fearful of the horse that I know is completely fine.

They'll walk into the ring and that horse is energetic as all get out. I can walk in there and get hold of that horse and everything is fine. They'll say, "Well, you've been working with him for the last fifteen days, so he's used to you. But he's not used to me because I've been gone." I'm like, you think this horse is really that turned up, that keyed up? I'll put my daughter Hensley at the end of that lead rope and that horse will drop his head and follow her around. And I mean she ain't been near that horse in fifteen days, she ain't been near that horse maybe at all. But she has no intent. She has no fear of it. She's just excited to lead a horse. So the emotional stuff that we put in there and the things that we get into our heads when we get in that heightened state, we become less aware. When horses get in that heightened state, they become more aware of what's around them.

Paul:

Your daughter has no baggage she is bringing to the relationship which is why the horses are at peace with her.

Dustin:

Exactly. Because, when humans get in a fearful state or they're worried about stuff the horse may do, they freeze and they don't really know what to do. But when a horse gets to that point, they know exactly what to do. They pick up on every little thing, and it's being able to control that, and know not to freeze and keep your emotions down. I mean, Aimee's seen it many times. I've had clients that are in the ring, and the horse is running off and about to buck them off. And I'll take a drink of coffee and walk in there real slow in the round pen and everybody panics, "Oh, my god, he's going to die." However, when I walk in there the horse will just slow down and come right over to me. So the owner really needs to change their energy and approach. While they're out there shaking to death, I never got worked up about it because I knew if I did when I got in there to take care of what was going on, things were going to be even worse. You've got to learn to stay even-keeled all the time and not get worked up. And that's easier said than done.

Paul:

We really have two different layers here. One is that when horses are fearful, suddenly they go into hyper decision-making mode. They analyze everything around them extremely quickly to figure out what their solution is as far as getting out of that situation.

Dustin:

Yes, because the self-preservation in the horse is very strong.

Paul:

And yet humans, when they are fearful, can suddenly become tunnel-blind. They can be paralyzed in their thinking and in their next movement because the fear is what's causing that. But then you're also saying on another level that if that's what we do as humans, that we know that when we're fearful we have this stress that paralyzes us mentally and physically, we should be able to self-regulate by saying, "OK, this is what's happening. I can feel it happening. I'm going to redirect my anxiety and I'm going to force myself into a different mental state so that I can lock into that self-awareness that's more acute." Whereas, a horse locks into that self-awareness right away. Very interesting.

Dustin:

I think I'm part horse because when everything starts to go south, I don't get worked up, I work through everything. I mean the defecation can hit the rotary oscillator, and I completely stay calm through everything, and everybody asks, "How the hell did you do that?" I don't know why but I've always been that way. I try and get people to be that way too, but I know it's tough. I've been in the middle of some really bad crap, and, if you lose your cool, you lose your mind, then you're over with. So I don't know, perhaps it's bred into you. I have no idea if it's a sixth sense or what.

Paul:

It could be a mix of things in how you've had to deal with life. You've had some adversity that you've had to work through, and had to make decisions to either succumb to those challenging problems or to say, "You know what, I'm just going to get back up." I guess that's where the expression "get back on the horse" comes from.

Dustin:
Yeah. Get back on that horse and ride again.

Connecting the Dots

Possessing emotional intelligence allows us to keep our ego in check. It produces a healthy ego where we feel good about ourselves and extend good will towards others. Simply stated, it is being aware of *being aware*. It is our internal motivation and regulation apparatus.

This is what we can learn from horses. They are extraordinarily aware of everything around them, including us humans with whom they interact. As Dustin revealed, "A horse is a mirror of you and your energy level." Even when stressed, horses become acutely focused, whereas humans tend to shut down and experience tunnel vision.

Being aware of ourselves and of others requires us to be centered. Centeredness requires mindfulness. According to expert Jeremy Hunter, mindfulness is our "...innate ability to be present, aware, and adaptable as we face the challenges of our busy lives." He goes on to state that, "Both science and experience demonstrate how being mindful brings positive benefits for our health, happiness, work, and relationships." All of these aspects are part of emotional intelligence.

There is no disputing that we cannot begin to understand others unless we intimately understand ourselves, and not just intellectually, but also emotionally. We need to understand what drives us. That will allow us to dream about and fully realize our own possibilities and purpose.

Cowboy-Conductor Challenge

If you are not self-aware, or disciplined in self-control, much less connected to others through emotional intelligence, it is very difficult to venture out on your own to improve yourself.

Choose someone you can trust with your most vulnerable self, perhaps a professional colleague, a personal friend, or life partner. Have them "spot you" as bodybuilders do in weightlifting. After all, you are developing this emotional intelligence muscle of yours. You want to be safe.

Remember the essence of emotional intelligence is self-awareness, self-regulation, internal motivation, empathy, and connectivity to others. As you are able, have your spotter observe your words and actions throughout the day. They will be looking for misplaced frustration, uncontrollable discord, oblivion, disconnection, if and how you support others, and how smoothly you deliver or bungle words and actions. You both might want to start with the obvious and work your way into the minutia, the microaggressions, as you progress down the road toward elevated emotional intelligence. Even better, you might want to serve as spotters for each other so it does not seem one-sided, as that could be a deterrent to continuing.

This experience will give you a heightened awareness of everything and everyone around you. You will become more attuned to what you say and do, as well as become keenly aware of others' verbal, physical, and emotional states.

How did you feel about the feedback you received?

Developing new or improving upon existing abilities takes time. Allow yourself the time necessary to solidly build a foundation. Let yourself sit in the grey. Like a pearl developing in an oyster, it can take as short as six months or as long as four years. Do not let the time it takes be a deterrent. Because once you do develop a well-grounded ability to call upon your emotional intelligence, anything is possible.

ON BEING CURIOUS

Saddling Up

The famous children's book and television series *Curious George*, by Margret and H.A. Rey, depicts the colorful and curious life of George, a monkey who lives in the big city and loves getting into anything and everything around him. Now, while most of his antics were outlandish, they seem to have a similar moral that being curious is a virtue and can lead you down paths you might not have chosen on your own, despite some mishaps along the way. In fact, in *Curious George Takes a Job*, he starts out washing dishes at a restaurant, then is hired to be a window cleaner for a tall apartment building, paints a penthouse apartment, gets chased by the owner who never wanted him to paint her apartment, breaks his leg running away, winds up in the hospital where he overdoses on ether, and then, of course, makes a movie of his life adventures and invites everyone in the town to its premiere. Totally normal. Right? At least in the world of curious it is.

Conversation

Dustin:

You seem to know a lot about self-awareness and motivation. Give me a better idea of what you're doing now and how you got so interested in that, and how it has turned into such a fulfilling professional career for you.

Paul:

Well, again, I've wandered through a lot of doors to get to where I am now. And looking back, there were moments that brought me here, but I didn't realize that until I looked back. It reminds me of the many jobs that I thought I was perfect for, in job searches where I had gotten to be one of two final candidates that they were considering hiring. And I wound up not getting them. Actually, one I did get, but a headhunter that same day said, "Hey, you should check out this other job before you accept the original one. It pays twice as much." So I did. And, of course, me saying to the original job search committee, "Just give me a week to sort something out," pissed them off and they pulled their job offer. I thank God they did because I would have been living in a place and wandering through a different set of doors that I probably wouldn't have liked.

Dustin:

Interesting.

Paul:

Looking back, it all makes sense. But sometimes when you're moving through doors or doors get slammed in your face, you think, "Wow, that was really unfair." That door was slammed, but it was slammed for good reason because another door was opening.

I grew up in Baltimore where we had row homes adjacent to each other. The skinny kind where if you reach your arms across the room, you can touch both walls. The row homes had these white marble steps that were famous in Baltimore at that time. They actually called them stoops. Neighbors would sit outside on their stoop after dinner and visit with each other. I used to walk up and down the street every night just talking to the neighbors and listening to their stories and getting to know them. I was curious about their lives. And as I look back now, that was really the nucleus for what I do today, which is literally trying to understand people and understand their motives, understand who they are and what their story is. And I realized then, as I do now, that there isn't just one way of looking at things.

So I put all of this into life's blender, this socializing, observational experience, and my entrepreneurial drive where I was always trying to make money and trying to figure out what the next best thing was or how I could do something that no one else had done before. Then add to that my journey into conducting. In our conducting lessons, we had to communicate without talking. All of this makes quite the blended drink, so to speak. At one end of the spectrum, I was a kid talking to everybody I could, and at the other end, I was learning how to communicate without talking and still getting the same results. And with the music, not only the piano and organ that I studied, but also with conducting and composing, there is the constant question of what's beyond the obvious? What's beyond the notes on the page? What is it trying to say? What's the theme? What's the story? What's the message? Connecting the dots. If I take all those things, those moments in my life and put them together, it's what I do today, which is walk into situations or organizations with some kind of conflict and figure out what's beyond the obvious. How can I connect the dots? How can we rearrange the notes to create a different composition here? What is the effect of people leading or leaving this organization? Who are they? What are their stories? What are their qualifications? What are they bringing to it? Are they helping or are they hindering the situation? I find the answers to all of those questions through present perception. Exactly what we talked about with horses. You walk into a herd of horses and you feel everyone out. You can't just walk in with your toolbox and say, "Well, this is the way it is." So I'm really assessing people's motives through non-verbal communication, and all that is very fascinating to me.

One other story about my past affecting my present is when I lived in Minneapolis for seven years. It would start snowing October first and we wouldn't see the snow melt until May, so it was a very long, cold winter. But thankfully, we had the Mall of America to go to. And the mall was huge. It was warm and it had an amusement park inside of it. You could actually go on a log ride in the middle of February, indoors, and get hotdogs and pretend you were at an amusement park! I'd spend a good amount of time there trying to get out of the snow and cold. What I loved to do was get an ice cream, sit on a bench, and watch people walk by and try to understand them and their motives. I realized the first time I did this that people actually circled the mall. They would circle three, four, ten times. I never knew people circled. I thought that they went and got their stuff and they left. But I just observed people. What shop did they wander into? When they made that lap, what did they buy? Why did they buy it? Why were they wearing the clothes they were wearing? Who were they with? Watching and studying people, and talking with people is fascinating, because we're such complex organisms, and there are certain motives and certain foundational things that we all have as part of being human. But just like the universe, there's a whole lot that's unknown. I know we've tried to nail down the physical, mental, and emotional things that we all have, but I think there's an infinite number of things that we just don't know about humans. Constantly fueling my curiosity is how I got here and it's what keeps me interested in what I do every day.

Dustin:

That's fascinating. It's interesting to me because people-watching is what I do all the time. Aimee's constantly reminding me, "You're great at it because no one knows you're watching them." It doesn't matter if we're at an airport, a restaurant, or wherever, I just enjoy watching people. It is so fascinating to me why people do what they do, the rhythms they get into, the comfort zones. It tells you a lot about people. And I think that's very helpful in my line of work, and I'm very sure it helps within your line of work. Because watching those mannerisms, watching what people do, you see their strengths. You find weak places. You find things you can build on and things that you need to remove out of situations, and it's the same with a horse. You find places that they're really strong. You find places that need to be better.

Paul:

I totally agree. I also love airports for that very reason. I'll sit down if I'm early and just watch people. It's fascinating. But you also said something that I think is important and tied to our success and who we are, which is that you are constantly aware of what's happening around you. I am the same. You mentioned the restaurant. Whoever is at the tables around me, I am listening and watching them, and I have a sense of what's happening in any given moment. And I'll say to my wife, "Did you hear that?" And she'll say, "What are you talking about?" And so I'll say, "Listen, there's something going on behind us." That awareness and peripheral vision is vital to understanding the world around you, not just seeing what is straight in front of you, which I think a lot of people do. They close off the world.

Dustin:

Oh, yeah. I'm very aware of what's going on around me to the point I'm so bad that usually if we go to a restaurant and we sit at a table where one chair is facing the door and one chair has got its back to the wall, I'll sit with my back to the wall. I do not like my back to a door. If I have to sit that way and there's a mirror, I know every reflective surface in that building and I know who's where and what's moving and what's going on. And I'm the same as you. We'll be sitting there, and I'll ask, "Did you hear what that lady said?" And Aimee will say, "What are you talking about?" And then I respond, "I cannot believe she just said that to her husband and her kids;" and I'll tell Aimee what she said. Then agitated, Aimee will ask, "Did you hear what I said?" And I counter, "Well, yeah, I heard what you said, but this is a whole lot more interesting than what you said." So, yes, I'm very aware of what's going on around me all the time, where people are, what's happening.

Paul:

I am always using my peripheral vision and hearing. And bringing it back to conducting, my grandmother used to always ask, "What are you doing up there? No one's watching you. Why are you even up there?" But musicians are always watching each other and watching  the conductor even though it looks like their heads are down in their music stands. There is a continual awareness of what's going on and a feeling about the moment. With conducting, you have eighty musicians seated in front of you. If that one person all the way in the back has an issue, you need to know that. You have to always be open to the slightest nuance.

Is this similar to how you work with horses?

Dustin:
Absolutely. Like I was telling you the other day when Marco was in the round pen with me and I was working with that one mare and she was jumping every which way; and, as we were going around, I'm telling him to get that rope unwrapped around his hand. And he said, "How did you ever see that with everything that was going on, with two horses in there moving around. One's running off and you're moving that horse and she's jerking you around. How did you ever know that I had a rope wrapped around my hand?" I'm always aware of what's around me, what's taking place.

Paul:
That kind of skill and approach can be life-saving.

Connecting the Dots

Paul's curiosity as a child visiting his neighbors on their Baltimore stoops every evening, and Dustin's curiosity about people everywhere he goes, combined with the nonverbal communication required by both of their jobs, led them to develop an approach of openness to situations and their solutions.

In some teachings and dogmas, curiosity is a bad thing. It can lead to serious trouble or unwanted outcomes, such as wondering about the secret ingredient in an exotic tostada only to find out that it is queen ant eggs. True story. However, fostering curiosity has been known to lead to greater creativity, imagination, and unusual ideas which can be very helpful in finding a solution that has yet to be realized for new and existing problems such as how can we travel faster and safer or contain a new global virus.

Being curious allows you to do what this section in every chapter is all about - connect the dots - to look beyond the obvious. Many times the dots are dispersed over a very large area. They usually do not present themselves in a neat and orderly fashion. You may pick up on a dot here today, and then not observe another useful dot for days or weeks. Dots come in all forms. They could be pieces of written data, verbal cues, facial micro-expressions or subtle body language, individual versions of people's experiences, or past wisdom overlaid with today's challenges. Identifying, analyzing, rearranging, and understanding what each dot means in the collective requires patience because you are exploring the nooks and crannies of nuance which takes time.

Of all the characteristics of a new hire or new relationship, curiosity should be a top priority to assess. If an employee is curious, that person will always be pushing the envelope to find answers to questions the organization may not even know exist. This leads to vision, strategy, and accomplishing the impossible. If a personal partner is curious, that person will continually bring a fresh, stimulating approach to the relationship which can lead to a never-ending physical, intellectual, and emotional journey.

Research has proven that curiosity generates dopamine triggering a euphoria which will fuel your desire to be even more curious. This will build on itself ad infinitum. This leads to happier, more intelligent, and more productive people which can have a direct effect on an organization's sustainable success. Curiosity is vastly underappreciated and underutilized which makes it our most powerful competitive advantage today.

Cowboy-Conductor Challenge

There is a whole book we could write on how to promote and nurture curiosity in your organization. Of utmost importance is that whatever you decide to do to foster curiosity, it must be embedded with authenticity. You must honestly believe in it and support it from your heart. People, like sharks to blood, will be able to smell your insincerity from miles away. We guarantee it.

Here are three ideas to get you started.

Whiteboard. A simple way to generate curiosity and creative thinking is to have a community whiteboard, perhaps located in a common area such as the break room, where, every day, people can participate in a provocative question by writing their answers for everyone to see. One question might be, "If a genie only gave you one wish, what would it be and why?" This approach alone can generate an environment of openness.

Why, Why, Why? Another possibility of generating curiosity within your organization is designing and implementing a monthly "Why?" brainstorming session for your team or the entire company if you dare. It sounds simple at first, but the answer to the first "Why?" will trigger a second "Why?" which then triggers the third "Why?" and so on. For instance, the first question could be, "Why does our company exist?" One of the answers might be, "To produce a superior wine" - a true story response from one of our past clients. To that answer, might come the next question, "Why should anyone care about imbibing a superior wine, especially at our price point?" The answer might be, "Because it naturally pairs with so many different dishes." Following that answer might prompt the question, "Why it is so important to pair wine with food anyway?" And so on. The more you ask the why to the why and drill down to the very essence of the original question, the closer you will get to the foundational answer, and thus the most impactful solution.

Design Thinking. A third approach, of the many we have used over the years, is adding a version of Design Thinking to your regular meetings. For example, at a monthly, dedicated think-tank session, you could identify a problem you are trying to solve. This might be a current or anticipated one. Then, have a free-form, no restrictions, brainstorming workshop to identify as many solutions as you can, choosing the best ones to pursue. Next, build a prototype of the absolute best solution. Do not worry about realistic barriers including time, money, or personnel. Test it out with the whole group. Listen for improvement suggestions. Then go back to the drawing board to creatively build upon what you know, what you believe to be true, and what feedback you were given. This exercise may or may not lead to a real solution of a real problem, but it will develop your organization's creative approach to obstacles.

While curiosity may have killed the cat, remember that it had a creative run of nine tries before getting there.

ON BEING PRESENT

Saddling Up

In his 1956 autobiographical book titled *The Walter Hagen Story*, celebrated American golfer Walter Charles Hagen wrote, "Don't hurry. Don't worry. And be sure to smell the flowers along the way." With the help of the 1974 title song, *Stop and Smell the Roses* by Mac Davis and Doc Severinsen, this has been a go-to phrase ever since. While a bit cliché, the saying implores us to be present. We all know that the past is past. You cannot do anything about it except learn from it. The future has not yet happened, so there is not anything to reflect upon. However, the present is all around us, begging to be noticed.

Conversation

Paul:

The peripheral vision we talked about earlier is a metaphor for being aware and comparing, listening, and observing. Are horses very similar that way? Are they always present? Are they constantly assessing and understanding what's going on even though they look like they are just having a fun time in the pasture?

Dustin:

Oh yeah, shoot, I've seen troubled horses even do it. I've seen horses that will take off bucking around when you saddle them for the first time, and they'll be troubled and scared, and there may be a flag or something that spooked them. I mean their heads are down and they are bucking hard and they are scared of something in front of them that jumps up and they will jump sideways and completely around it. They are that aware of what's going on around them. And there's times that they'll run into fences and different things because they're so scared as well, but you see both sides of it. It just depends how scared that horse is. I've got a grey horse that doesn't miss a thing. I mean that horse you can ride him across the pasture and the littlest thing like a bird or a lizard can just move off to his right side and he'll just sidestep over and you think, "What was that all about!" You look down and you'll see that little lizard or field mouse. You're thinking, "I didn't see that, but he caught it." He was more aware than I was. Some horses are more sensitive and more aware than others. I've got another gelding that I'm pretty sure nothing would faze him. You could blow a bomb up in front of him and he'd be like, "Huh?" He'd never see it coming. And, it's just who he is. He's always been that way. But I think there's a lot of people who walk through life that way too. They don't have a clue that anything could ever possibly happen - and then it does.

Paul:

Yeah, it's amazing to me. Being present is really important. If you can practice being present, to boost your awareness, that's important. But even when talking with others we tend to not really listen. We're just waiting for our turn to speak as opposed to truly listening and reacting to what that person says. So even simple things like being present during a conversation is vital, not to mention driving and looking at your phone when you're going sixty-five miles an hour on the highway.

You also mentioned that you are always aware of what's happening. You're always watching or assessing. That is really important because on the business side, people are watching and comparing and trying to figure out how you're treating their peer, how you're treating their subordinate, how you're treating their leaders. They may not always tell you they're watching or listening, but they're constantly comparing and watching and observing you and your leadership and how each is being treated. One cannot underestimate the impact this has on a company, on a herd.

Dustin:

I've noticed that too. I think a lot of people nowadays don't listen with the intent to hear; they listen with the intent to respond. I find myself, when I'm in those situations with somebody like this, and I'll be speaking with them and they respond, "Oh, yeah," I'll just rephrase exactly what I said, but then I'll end it in a question. That always catches them off guard. They'll look at you puzzled and think for a second. I'll then ask, "Do you understand what I'm saying?" And they look at you, and they say, "No." And I think to myself, "Well, you didn't understand me the first time either because you popped right back off." You gotta listen with the intent to understand, not to respond. Because if I listened to my horses with the intent to just respond, that would simply be a reaction to an action. But if I listen with the intent to respond with something that would help that horse, or if that horse was troubled and I was listening in a way where I was present, where I can help that horse get out of trouble, then that's what's important. I'm not watching that horse and reacting. I'm there to understand what the horse needs or what he is asking me and help him work through that, not my preconceived response to what I think he needs.

And I think if people could learn that, especially with their children, man, the world would be a whole lot better.

Paul:

Yeah, it really is all about listening and authentically being present. You know that famous phrase, "You have two ears and one mouth for a reason, to listen twice as much as you speak." And you're right. It goes beyond that because, as you said, you can listen and hear what they say, but are you really absorbing what they say or are you just listening to words going in your funnels? Because what you say back to me then determines whether you actually heard me. That also gives you insight into people's motives and leadership as well. If you have someone who will listen to you for half an hour and then say something that's totally different than what you were talking to them about, you know they weren't really listening. Or, they were listening, but they weren't really understanding or caring about what you were saying. Subtlety matters. It speaks volumes, so to say.

Dustin:
Completely.

Connecting the Dots

It is absolutely true that we do not listen. But why? Because we love talking about ourselves. And why not? We are fabulous! Or, are we addicted?

Researchers from the Harvard University of Social Cognitive and Affective Neuroscience Lab identified two regions of the brain never before associated with our pleasure of talking about ourselves, the nucleus accumbens and the ventral tegmental area. Both parts of the mesolimbic dopamine system are associated with reward, and linked to pleasurable feelings and motivational states associated with stimuli such as sex, cocaine, and good food. This research suggests we cannot help but talk about ourselves, despite how interesting other topics might be because it gives us such compulsive pleasure. However, this behavior is not only enslaving, it also signals to others what we value. We must strive to, "Listen with the intent to understand, not to respond," as Dustin so eloquently suggests.

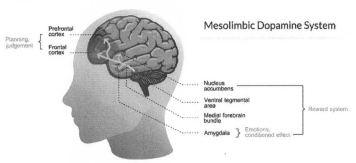

We need to be present not only in words, but also in actions - focused, not distracted. In 2009, Basex Inc. wrote a case study about Intel Corporation's war on information overload. In it, they stated that unnecessary interruptions, plus the time it takes a knowledge worker to get back to where they were before, consumes an average of twenty-eight percent of a knowledge worker's day, or a disturbing thirty-six billion wasted person-hours each year in the United States alone!

Our distraction is not only wasteful, it can be deadly. Think about it. When you drive on the highway at sixty-five miles an hour while texting, that equals not looking up for an entire length of a football field while you spend those seemingly short four seconds sending a response to friends about how much you enjoyed the photo of their frothy, heart-designed lattes.

The obsession over self-disclosure mixed with addictive

social media behavior spells disaster for your work, for your relationships, and for yourself. You can counter this by forcing yourself to be present. This will not only decrease your destructive behavior, it might even save someone's life. Yours.

Cowboy-Conductor Challenge

Mindfulness is the new silver bullet. Why not give it a shot?

Being present. Find a place to sit down, any place. Contrary to other mindfulness exercises, this place does not have to be in a quiet, uninterrupted location. Sit down with both of your feet flat on the ground, your butt fully engaged in your seat, and your eyes completely closed. Feel the energy between your feet and the ground as well as your body's points of contact with the chair. Once you feel grounded, listen. At first, you might hear only the loudest sounds. Listen further. What distant sounds do you hear now? Next, smell. What pungent aromas do you detect? Take a slow, deep breath. What faint smells can you identify? Focus on how these sensations, large or small, make the inside of your brain feel. How do they make the innards of your stomach feel? What are your toes feeling? There is no right or wrong answer. Being aware enough to be able to answer these questions is all that matters. This is being present.

Listen to hear. At work, train yourself to, as Dustin

says, "listen to hear" when a colleague stops by your desk or calls you on the phone. When this happens, completely stop what you are doing. Take a moment to transition out of your task. Next, turn your body to face your colleague and look directly at them while firmly planting your feet on the floor to ground yourself. Close out the rest of the world beyond the two of you. Then, focus on each word, each thought, and each intention. When they have come to a pause in their message and before you add to the conversation, take a few seconds to figuratively chew on and digest what you have heard before you add to the dialogue. Slowing the pace of the conversation alone will assist you in being present. It will center you, even if for a brief moment, and allow you to fully engage.

If you always make it a rule to listen twice as much as you speak, you will gain a deeper understanding of the world around you, and exude a natural compassion that others will treasure.

ON VERBAL INTENTION

Saddling Up

Have you ever experienced a heavy snowstorm with thick flakes falling from the sky? Soon after it finishes and you are out in it alone, what do you hear? Absolute silence. A deafening silence that seems void of life. To some, this experience is comforting. To others, it is terrifying. That is exactly why knowing your audience and *how* you use sound makes a difference in the response you get from others. Is it loud, quiet, high, low, boisterous, sheepish, angry, or excited? While body language and facial expressions round out your delivery, the use of verbal cues is paramount to your intent. And *intent* is what you are ultimately judged on.

Conversation

Paul:

I know this sounds like a strange question, but we've been talking a lot about the many types of non-verbal communication. But with verbal communication, do horses actually respond to words, to pitches, to phrases like dogs do? Dogs seem to know their name and words such as "come," "dinner," "food," or the ever-popular "treat." Dogs respond to all of those. Do horses similarly respond to words or pitches, to verbal communication?

Dustin:

They do. My great grandfather was a hell of a teamster. I've got pictures of him in Walla Walla, Washington. He's got sixty-four head of horses in his hands cutting wheat on the threshing machine. And it's all about "gee" and "haw;" that's how they got them horses left and right. "Get-up" and "woah." Now that's for driving horses in teams. When we're driving the miniatures, we'll cluck and kiss. Although, I've got a couple of them that I've started that I don't really cluck or kiss to. I may cluck to get them up, but then I'll use my body position in the cart to move them like I would if I was on a saddle horse. And Aimee told me when I first got around to driving miniatures, this is just what we do. And I've never clucked and kissed before in my life. That just wasn't part of what we did. If you did that, you weren't a very good hand where I was raised. But you get around the horse show world and, Jiminy

Christmas, you get around one of them arenas and "cluck, cluck, cluck, cluck, cluck." Everybody's clucking and kissing.

Paul:

Do horses respond to that? Or do we think they do?

Dustin:

Yes, but only if you use it correctly. But most people overuse it. If I was asking my horse to do something, like move up to the trot, I would ask him with a cluck. And if I didn't get a response I would cluck again and follow up with one of my training aids and if he trotted off that's great. But what you find is people cluck and they cluck and they cluck and they cluck, and then they reinforce it, *but* they stay clucking and clucking and clucking. Then pretty soon the cluck means nothing. And then you've taught that horse to just ignore the cluck. You're doing it strictly for yourself. It doesn't do you any good. Now some people have figured out how to use "woah" to make one stop and get its ass in the dirt. When they say "woah," a horse will flat stop, but they haven't figured out how to use the cluck and the kiss to get a horse to go because it's just a constant that they overuse; it becomes white noise to the horse. The guys I ride with and the people I've been around, you won't hear them clucking and kissing. And if you do, they're gonna look at you, like, "What the hell is wrong with you!" There's a better way to get along with your horse. And Aimee's got one older gelding that she can do everything with him just off of clucks and kisses and body positioning and he's right there.

It's pretty funny because when we hire people, you can

tell the cluckers and the kissers right away. I mean the first two weeks, they gotta hate me, because I tell them, "If you do it one more time...!" I'll finally get to the point where I say, "Every time I hear you cluck and kiss, I'm docking $100 off your pay!" Usually, that stops them pretty quick. And I've never had one try me on that, thank God. Now I probably will have them challenge me once this hits publication. But they'll come in here and I'll tell them, "You can't do that all the time because it is such a valuable tool if used correctly." If you do it right, that horse knows when you cluck he needs to hit a trot in the cart. But if every time you walk him out of his stall, you cluck to him, what's it going to mean to him when I get him in the cart? Doesn't mean nothing. So, it'd be like telling your kid, "Hey, get up and get the trash, get up and get the trash, get up and get the trash!" Pretty soon, after you've told him a hundred times, he still ain't got the trash. You just taught him to ignore you. Now if I say, "Get up and get the trash" a second time and then I have him by the ear, and I'm gonna help him get that trash, and then we're going to do it together. Now that's intentional. Next time I probably won't have to ask twice.

Paul:
Yeah, you bring up an excellent point. It's a great transition because it's the same with leadership. Two things actually come to mind. One is using your words and choosing your words carefully, and the second is knowing when and how to use inflection, how you use pitches and sound. If you say the same things with the same energy all the time to everyone who's in front of you, then people are going to realize you've got this rote thing going as opposed

to intentionally communicating with different people at different times in different styles. You need to meet them where they are and understand how you need to communicate with that particular person. I imagine the clucking and kissing and body movement works with some, but it doesn't work with all. And yet, we still think, "Well, it worked with this one, it's gotta work with everybody else so let's just keep clucking and kissing 'til I'm dead, or 'til I'm hoarse," so to speak. And it's the same thing with kids and with employees. Not everything works the same with everyone. For instance, there are people who are more sensitive to all capital letters in an email. People say that's harassment if you put everything in capitals because you're yelling at them through an email. And some people I know write all capitals just because that's what they do. It's their regular style. So there's this idea we talked about a lot, about listening. But I think talking and approaching people with carefully chosen words also matters. You have to have a wide variety of inflections and vocabulary to be able to truly make a difference.

Dustin:

I agree. You can tell around here when I've gotten upset, and there ain't a person in this place that doesn't know it when I've hit my breaking point. Everybody knows because everything changes. My walk changes, my body position changes, my words change, my tone changes. And if I'm trying to drive home a point, I can't just be monotone. Just like with a horse, I try and dial it up and dial it back down. So I do the same thing with myself all the time. And you bring up another interesting point to me because we've also found, especially with the younger folks that we've hired, that if you send something in all capitals, they take offense to it like you're yelling at 'em.

That's kinda the same as these horses that have been prodded along the whole lot, or not prodded, they'd been catered to their whole life and they've been raised almost like a spoiled child where they learn to walk all over you. It's kind of like somebody's younger kids coming up in the world that have gotten participation ribbons for everything. And they almost become uncoachable, to where you can't say, "Hey, that was wrong and you need to fix it." Because, it's like you said, they'll respond with, "Oh my God, that's harassment!" They think you yelled at them and they can't handle it. That goes back on their parents, and I have the same issues with horse owners. I tell them, "This is no different than your child, and I'll bet your child's this way." There's been a few of those parents that finally realize, "Yeah, my kid does act like that." I'll say, "Well then how do you think your horse was going to act with you any differently?" So, like you said, one, you've gotta get a little thicker skin in life, and two, you've got to be able to not only accept those things when someone has changed their voice as an employee, but as a leader you need to be able to adjust yourself so that it's not monotone every time you speak.

So it's a big thing, and it's funny you say the quiet thing, though, to jump back to that real quick. We had some girls working for us and things were going crazy one day and I was mad. And then I got dead silent for a while. Marco finally came to me and he said, "What's going on?" I said, "You ever heard the old saying about 'watch the quiet one?'" He said, "No, what's that mean?" I said,

"When that guy gets quiet watch out because he's fixin' to cut fence and sort some shit out and I am fixing to do it right now." And he panicked and said, "Oh hell!" That poor kid turned ghostly white. He asked, "Am I in trouble?" I said "You're not, but there's some others that are fixin' to get in a lot of trouble." Sometimes that quiet guy can be a really bad thing around here, let me tell you.

Paul:
Exactly! Because, then, when you adjust your message and are intentional about it, it can have a much bigger impact. If you were to just yell and scream and stomp around all the time, after a few days your employees would say, "Oh, that's just Dustin being Dustin." And where would you go from there? There's no impactful moment. Now that moment may be just the opposite, right? So, if you're always yelling and screaming and then, all of a sudden, you become eerily quiet, and you use that for effect, then they might say, "Uh oh, something's happening, Dustin's quiet." I think, whatever your stance is, you've got to be able to, as you said, dial it up and dial it back to meet the moment so that people know when there has been a change. So many folks use the same monotone voice whether it's loud or soft or medium. It doesn't work.

You also bring up another point that I believe in, which is how parents are raising their kids now will affect the workplace in twenty years. And if you think about it and what that workplace culture will look like in twenty years, that's a big responsibility. So they're not only raising their kids, they're raising the next generation of business and world leaders.

Dustin:

That's a whole other book in itself.

Connecting the Dots

Think about the use of music in a movie. Is the music quiet and soothing? Is it loud and agitated? Is it slow and pensive? Is it fast and exuberant? The timbre of the music gives insight as to the intention of the scene. Take, for instance, a person running down the middle of the street. Is the music menacing, signaling the person is running from a murderer? Or is the music exhilarating, signaling a breakthrough accomplishment or end of a lifelong marathon of sorts? The scene without the music overlay represents the words you use, the content. The overlaid score represents intent.

You must meet people where they are and bring them along from there. If you start on a different verbal plane than the person with whom you are speaking, not only will your message be lost, it may also be dreadfully misinterpreted, causing great harm to both of you.

Now more than ever before, people are extremely sensitive not only to what you say to them, but also how you say it. Those who were raised primarily on praise and sweet talk are particularly delicate to even a hint of authority or self-assuredness in verbal cues. They often take it as a threat or harassment. In a period of litigious pervasiveness, you must choose your words and sounds carefully, or face unintended consequences.

Organizations tend to settle legal challenges instead of defending themselves, despite their innocence, because it is more cost-effective than a full-blown trial. Therefore, how you address or respond to your colleagues could find you on the other side of justice or out of a job.

Carefully choose your words. Carefully choose your tone. Delight in the response you receive!

Cowboy-Conductor Challenge

The majority of us have not had formal training in the art of speech delivery. We usually develop our professional skills through the past-lessons-learned method. This can be dangerous. There are many organizations in which you can enlist, such as Toastmasters International®, to help you improve the effectiveness and intention of what comes out of your mouth. You can also improve verbal and written intentions immediately in simple, practical ways using our authentic approach to enhancing your skills.

Deliver an impactful email. First, write it all out. Walk away from it for a few hours. Reread it. Have someone you trust read it and summarize what they think your intention is to see if it matches what you had in mind. Make the edits. Walk away again for a time. Reread it. If you feel that every word can be defended as to intent, send it. If not, go back and adjust.

Deliver a critical message in person. First, write it all

out. Walk away from it for a few hours. Reread it. Have someone you trust listen to you deliver it to them as the planned audience and then summarize what they think you intended to say to see if it matches what you had in mind. Make the edits. Walk away again for a time. Deliver the message again to your trusted colleague. Once you feel the message and the tone are defensible, deliver it.

How did it feel to deliver that message? Relief or complete dread? And more importantly, how did the other person feel? Fairly treated or harassed?

Remember, it is critical to meet others where they are intellectually, emotionally, and even physically. What you say, how you say it, and even where you say it matters. Deliver your message in a manner that is easily understood on first reading or hearing. Be sure to match your delivery to the recipient's normal or current emotional state. In other words, are they about to be fired and are expecting it, or are you giving them a promotion they have wanted for some time? Finally, where you deliver the message is paramount. If you are firing someone, do you choose a corporate setting such as the conference room or your office, or do you do it via email or letter? And if you are promoting someone to their dream job, do you choose a fancy restaurant or the local food truck? Do not underestimate that those who are on the receiving end of your messages are hyper-attuned to the what, the how, and the where.

If you are verbally intentional and sensitive to those with whom you are interacting, you increase your chances of them not killing the messenger. However, always remember that what you say – and more importantly, *how* you say it – can and may be used against you in a court of law.

ON WHAT'S IN IT FOR ME

Saddling Up

As a young child, how many times when your parents came home from the store with packages in tow did you excitedly ask, "What's for me? What's for me!" Fast forward to today when your company announces new changes that will make it even more successful. Is the first thing to pop into your head an excited "What's in it for me!" full of anticipation of a raise or better working conditions, or is it a resigned, "Ok. That's fine. But. What's in it for me?" while you contemplate if your job will still exist after the company's changes have been implemented? This last chapter explores this simple yet profound, egocentric question, "What's in it for me?" and how it can help or hinder your leadership.

Conversation

Paul:

You were talking about self-awareness, regulation, and motivation. I'm trained in change management methodology. Successful change management helps get people to move from their present state to a future state without them feeling like they were dragged there against their will.

Humans don't like change. Even if it's better for us, we tend not to like change. We don't like disruption, even a small change such as when you are on your way to work and have to take a half-block detour. We tend to get all pissed off about that and it ruins our next four hours. Even though this half-block is probably thirty seconds more out of our day, our commute, we're just in a twist about it. The change management methodology I use called Prosci®, which stands for professional science, has studied the change process of thousands and thousands of companies over many decades. They figure out best practices and how to get large numbers of people moving in a different direction as smoothly as possible so that they adapt to the new change as quickly as possible. Because if they don't adapt to whatever the new change is, usually that's time lost, money lost, and people lost. One method of change management in Prosci® is a process called ADKAR, which is an acronym for Awareness, Desire, Knowledge, Ability, and Reinforcement.

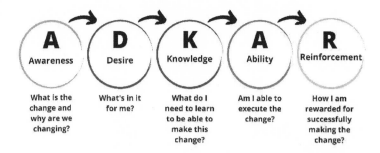

The first hurdle is awareness. People have to understand why the change is happening. What is the change? What's the reason for the change? And I don't mean, "We're going to go this more efficient and effective direction so follow us." There has to be a fully developed communication plan so that every single person is aware of what's happening.

But the second piece is really what I want to get to: desire. People want to know, "What's in it for me?" You must answer that for them if you want to make any progress. And that answer cannot just be that the company is going to be more successful and that they're going to get paid more money. That's not what's in it for them. It has to be something much more visceral, something more internal to who they are as a person. But if you can answer the "what's in it for them" question, usually you can get people to buy into it. Once you get them there, it's really a matter of teaching them and getting them up to speed on what the change is. But often we get stuck in either awareness or desire: (a) I don't know what this is about so how can I even get on board with it? or, (b) I understand, but why does it matter to me? What am I going to get out of it?

Is there anything to that with training horses? And is there a similar process of making them aware of what the problem is or change is, or where you want them to be, and get them to buy into it?

Dustin:
Well, I'll try to think how I can answer that one.

Paul:
Maybe the last three stages of ADKAR are more relevant. Knowledge. You're teaching them what they need to learn.

Dustin:
Right.

Paul:
Ability. Making sure that they can replicate whatever you've been teaching them so they can do it on their own.

Dustin:
Yes.

Paul:
Reinforcement. I'm sure you do that. There's got to be some kind of reinforcement for the knowledge and the ability that they've learned and are doing successfully.

So those three pieces of ADKAR are probably part of your every day because you're teaching them. But is there anything to this awareness and desire - convincing a horse to buy into your teaching them, your changing them?

Dustin:
Well, yeah, I think there is.

Paul:

Do you have to convince a horse?

Dustin:

You don't have to convince a horse, because a horse is very willing and they want to get along. But at the same time, you have to have that horse aware of you before you can teach that horse. And when I say that, you may have somebody trying to teach a horse something, and the horse is looking over yonder, they aren't in a learning state of mind. So, first, you need to know that you have that horse's attention and that the horse is aware of you, and aware that something's going to take place.

Paul:

Exactly. Awareness is the first step in the ADKAR process.

Dustin:

I'll use backing up off of a halter rope for example. You may start it off with your hand underneath the halter. At first, you would start like you're just gonna pick a little flower. You just are super light to see if that horse would take any part of that deal. And if he wouldn't, then you might firm up just a little bit, and a little bit more until you see the horse's mind start to think about it, then you'd quit. Most people don't see that. They're not going to quit until that horse moves. Well, you missed the first try that horse gave you. He tried when he thought about moving. Now, that was the first problem, the first thought and the first part of that move.

It's kinda like, if I told you, "Paul, take your hand down

off your chin." Well, first, you gotta think in your head, I gotta move my hand before I can take it off my chin, right? That was the first thing that went to your head. Even though, subconsciously, it didn't because it's just a natural move, right? But consciously that was the first thing you had to do is think that before you could do that. And then when you thought about it again, I might hold it for just a tick longer, and you might shift your weight.

And when that horse shifted his weight, then I'd go back and replicate that again. And I'd put that same little feel, like I was going to pick a flower, and he'd shift his weight. He'd think about it, he would shift his weight, he might lift his hoof, and I'd quit. Then pretty soon, we just keep building on that, and we'd keep replicating that 'til he's starting to back up, and then I'd just rub on him, and say, "Hey, that's really good," and we'd just be done with it for a while. We'd go on to something else.

Then, the reinforcement would come, because, later, I'd come back and I'd check that out again and say, "Hey, how little would it take for you?" The feel is really important. Feel is something that has a million different meanings. You can walk up there and just think about pushing that halter rope back, and them horses will just glide backwards. You don't even touch it. You just think about it. And they're already backing up. And that horse wants to backup for me. He can feel that. He's working for me. And he's doing it to please me. And then you see someone over there, and they're jerking their horse backwards and you think, "Do they even have a clue? Is there even a clue in their mind that there's something more there?"

Paul:

I think it is the same. For horses, the awareness comes from the leader who's trying to train the horse or, in my case, change the people. There has to be an awareness of how that horse or how that person is feeling and how they're reacting to you. So that awareness is a little different than what I talked about. But there is this desire piece from the horse that almost seems like a trust and respect issue we keep coming back to.

Dustin:

It is.

Paul:

If the horse doesn't trust you, or thinks you're an idiot, then it doesn't matter how you're approaching it because he or she doesn't want to buy into your idea. Humans are the same way.

Actually, part of change management data shows that if a change management project has a sponsor, somebody who's a respected and trusted decision maker either in that team or in that company, say the CEO or the head of a department, who says to everyone involved, "This is a great change and I stand behind it," then your chances of success go up threefold, especially if that sponsor is engaged throughout the entire process.

Dustin:

Oh, wow.

Paul:

The other thing you said that is interesting to me is that the horse teaches you. You must listen to what the horse has to say in order for you to then change how you're going to approach it or switch up your approach to it. That's very similar to how we get people past this desire hurdle and get people to buy into the change. There are strategically scheduled moments during a change management process where we administer surveys to ask them, "What do you know about this change?" and "How are you are feeling about this change?" If you can understand their viewpoint, you can address their concerns and help them move past those road blocks. But if you just say, "Damn it. Let's just go, we're doing this, okay?" it's guaranteed to fail. In the military, for instance, there wasn't much of a warm and fuzzy approach to getting people to move along in a way that it feels like it's their own idea. The military approach to change management used to be: "Just do it. Do you want a paycheck next week? Then that's your reinforcement." This is a reasonable approach in the military because, just as the lead mare alerts the herd of a threat, in the military everyone has to move along immediately after getting the warning or they risk being compromised or even killed.

Dustin:
Exactly.

Paul:
Convincing people to change requires emotional intelligence. You have to read people. You have to understand people and then react to them. It's the same thing in orchestras. You have to read the room, read the stage. You have to know all of what's happening to be able to decide, "OK, I'm just going to leave that there." Because, after

reading the stage full of musicians in real time, you may realize they are not going to hear what you want to tell them based on what you're feeling and what you're seeing in their body language. Maybe the next day they're more open to it, and then you address that issue because you feel more openness in the room with these eighty people. I think the same thing is true for teams. So many leaders want to have a cookie-cutter approach to how they move people through life, through the company, through a project as opposed to custom creating a useful approach.

I've been criticized since the very beginning of my career by some of my colleagues who say, "You can't just coddle people." But I don't think it's coddling. I think it's meeting every single person where they are, figuring out what they need and then stepping back and addressing how to meet that individual's needs within the group's needs to move everyone forward. You may have one-hundred head of horses, and you need to know every single one of them, what they need and what they don't need. At the same time, you must step back and figure out how to collectively manage that entire herd of horses. The more we can get into this deeper, detailed level of management and understanding of each other and how to motivate each other, that is what's going to be more successful than just charging that hill, and certainly less painful for everyone.

Dustin:

Exactly. What I tell everybody that works for us or handles our horses is, "If there are ninety head of horses, there are ninety personalities. What works for one isn't gonna work for the rest of them. Yet, there are a lot of different trainers out there that will say, "You got a horse with a certain pedigree. I won't take that horse. I don't work with that bloodline," because the trainer can't get along with them or they don't like them for whatever reason. But maybe if he would try and meet the horse where it is and bring it along, he could produce a world champion out of that horse. But these kinds of trainers don't know how to adjust their training to every unique horse they meet. But, for me, I adjust. My mentor, Ray, went all over the world and said he never found a horse that his methods didn't fit because he was always working from where the horse was at. He never found a horse he couldn't get along with. You think about that with humans. If you can go all over the world and never find anybody that you couldn't find a way to get along with, how cool would that be? How cool would that be to know you could just make it work? Whatever it was. There's always a way to get along.

Paul:

There are people who think that that's a sign of weakness because you are seen as a chameleon, that you are adapting to someone else's life, someone else's beliefs. They think you should stand firm in what you believe, who you are, and how you operate as opposed to getting along with everyone.

Dustin:

You can stand firm in your beliefs and someone else can stand firm in theirs. You're both entitled to your beliefs; it doesn't mean you have to agree. You can agree to disagree, but you can still get along. That's the division of Western civilization right now. No one thinks we can get along. I mean, look at the election right now. If you're for that candidate, then you're a sorry piece of...! Well, guess what? You've got your reasons for liking that guy. I got my reasons for liking this guy. We can still get along. We can still go have dinner together. We can have a drink together. We don't have to talk about politics. We can talk about how the weather is. We can talk about whatever, but people, they can't seem to get past their opinion. And if you can't see past your opinion, then you are a very small-minded, close-minded person.

Just because you're getting along with people doesn't mean you're a chameleon. I get along with a lot of people. And if you like me, great. If you don't like me, I guess that's kinda your problem, not mine because I'm entitled to my opinions and the way I live my life the same as you're entitled to yours. Could we find a way to still exist together? You bet we could. Doesn't mean we have to hate each other. But if someone said to me that I'm living a chameleon life because I get along with people, I mean, shit, let's talk about a chameleon life. I'm the only son of a buck within an I don't know how many miles' radius of where I live that dresses like the cowboy I am. I'm the only one in this town, but I get along with everyone just fine. I'm surrounded by all kinds of cultures, ethnicities, religions, every other person you can think of. I'm not getting bullied. I'm not a chameleon. I go to the grocery store and see who I can move. I'm not prejudiced. I move everybody, and I move out of the way for everybody. So why can't we all get along? Everyone is entitled to their opinions, the same as I am.

Paul:
People probably move out of your way at the grocery store because you're moving down the aisle riding your horse!

Dustin:
I wish I could. I would if they let me.

Paul:
I think this all goes back to being centered.

We seem to have come full circle: the herd mentality, the horses being equal, feeling centered in who they are, and how they move through life. And if we as humans could have some piece of that where we felt centered, then we wouldn't feel the need to move other people out of the way. That stepping aside in a grocery aisle is actually more a sign of power than it is a sign of weakness.

Dustin:
Exactly.

Paul:
We choose that consciously. Because as you said, you'd step out of the way for an old lady, but that's out of respect and that's a decision you decided to make, not because you were rolled over by that eighty-nine-year-old. It goes back to centeredness which has to do with emotional intelligence. It has to do with herd mentality. It has to do with the idea that how you change people is by this unspoken presence, posture, and palpable awareness. All of this is baked into our daily decision making, and yet we don't realize how both complicated and simple it is.

Dustin:

Right. And the worst part about the whole deal is that the human normally makes it tenfold harder than it actually is. Why? I don't know. Things are really pretty simple, and there's some grey areas in life. I understand that. But the biggest thing is you've got choices. How you make your choices is how things are going to play out for you. That's completely on you. That's on nobody else. Not your horse. Not your team member. But now we seem to be at a place in society where people blame everybody else for their own personal choices, and we're really getting into a twisted world that we shouldn't be in. You shouldn't blame somebody else for the choice you made. It's just not how it should work.

Paul:

But it's so much simpler to blame someone else. Then there's no accountability. It's gloriously easy!

Dustin:

Oh, it's incredibly easy. Everybody's looking for that painless way out. It reminds me of a saying, "Life is like a mountain. Hard to climb, but once you reach the top, the view is amazing." You can look at it one of two ways. Either it's going to be a terrible, long climb or you can say, "Hey, I like to climb. I'm gonna take it one step at a time and make it to the top." It doesn't say you have to do it all in one day. Just like the old saying about how to eat an elephant, one bite at a time. It may take me a while, but I'm still gonna get the whole thing eaten just the same as the guy that's trying to shove it down his throat all at once. Doesn't matter how you do it, you just have to consciously make the choices that fit you.

Paul:

Right. And we're the ones who put those restrictions on ourselves. Those barriers.

And, as you say, we create more complexity than there needs to be. I think life is complex enough, and the things we have to deal with and move through are tough enough without us putting our own personal layer of complexity and anxiety on top of that.

Dustin:

Oh yeah, and like you said, if you're going to work and there's a small detour, you gotta go around the one-half block, so what if it takes an extra thirty seconds out of your day? Most people get upset about that, and to me, well, what are you gonna do? It's life. It is what it is. You laugh about it and you take the detour. What else can you do? You can't will the situation away.

Paul:

Leadership comes from within, because to make that decision or to redirect that frustration from within actually makes you a better, more respected leader than unleashing your personal frustration on everybody that you meet in the next two hours of being pissed off. It actually takes more discipline and more resilience. And to me, that's what leadership is. It's redirecting that and not spewing emotional garbage over everyone you meet because you couldn't handle a little detour.

Dustin:

Shoot, if you let a little detour disturb you that badly and get your feathers all ruffled up, hell, I wouldn't want to be around you anyways.

Paul:

Exactly. What are they going to do when a real crisis happens?

Dustin:

You know, I've learned a lot of that patience through life, and a lot of that came from training horses. With every horse, I think about what I want to get done today. Here's where I want to start, this is where my training progress is gonna go for the day, and that's where I'm going to finish.

I look at life's progression like this straight arrow.

However, when it comes to working with horses in their natural state, the reality is that it usually looks more like this squirrely arrow.

So you have to adjust to fit every situation, but you can still end up at the same spot. It just may take a different route to get there. Who cares? You adjust to fit the horse; you adjust to fit the situation to where it helps both of you succeed. So big deal something went a little wrong. You just need to get a little creative and think of something different and you're still going to end up at the same successful spot. But for some reason, people can't get out of that one-channeled mind. This is how it's got to be.

Well, who knows? Maybe on that little detour, something came into your mind that gave you an idea that was great for a pitch at work. Who knows what could happen in that thirty seconds. But if you're pissed off at the world because you had a detour, what are you gonna get out of it? Nothing. Because then you're gonna lose time instead of actually gain time, or get something good out of life. So, to me, I learned to take it as it comes. Things are going to happen. One thing I've learned about horses, livestock, or whatever else, is that you can have the best laid plans in the world, but they are going to mess them up every time. It's part of life and you simply have to adjust to it.

Paul:

What's so ironically funny about your passionate speech just now is that we've talked about how you don't like to operate in the grey, and yet grey is everything you've just described to me.

Dustin:

I guess I do operate in the grey, probably all of the time.

Paul:

Hilarious! You have to own it. You are a grey leader.

Dustin:

That's fair to say. But, for me, I have to operate in that grey zone to figure out where that horse is so that horse can learn what's black and what's white. Because the horse is in the grey. That horse may think, "Well, I can push on this human." Well, then I have to operate there for a little bit, but over time that horse is going to learn that *I'm* the lead horse and he is down one on the pecking order from me. Because that's how it works in their environment. That's how their herd structure works. And so, therefore, you know, you can watch the lead horse in any herd and he or she could be standing there and another horse walks up there, and they're getting a drink, and all they got to do is pin an ear back, and that other horse will leave the water tank. And that's enough for them to tell that other horse, "You just wait your turn." But the human may not have caught that. They may have waited for the other horse to get up there to get a drink, and then they get big and they want to whack them and do all this other stuff. And it's like, no, you shouldn't. You should have picked up on something a whole lot subtler, a whole lot sooner.

Doing less sooner seems to get you a whole lot farther than doing a whole lot more later. It can cause a big wreck for everybody. So sometimes you have to operate through that grey, so that you can find a place to operate in black and white.

And the horse will learn pretty quick that I don't push you, and it's happened here a million times. We have horses right now that are our horses. They know when me and Aimee get a hold of them, we're the lead horse. But then, someone else who handles them for us and turns them out every day, they push and walk all over them. But then we can walk right up there and it's like, boy, that horse just comes right to attention, and they know this is how it needs to be. So they're like us, they learn what they can push on and what they can't.

Paul:

That's what a great leader does. They work in the grey and not just say, "Damn it, this is my formula, and this is how it works, and it has to work for everybody," because you must always be answering the question, "What's in it for me?" for those you are leading.

Dustin:

Right, because you have to adjust to what's in front of you, what you're working on at that moment and adjust to fit the situation.

So, I guess I really am a grey leader.

Paul:

A lot of people are not comfortable in grey. And in my personal opinion, I think that's why we have all the different belief systems. They help us through the unknown. There are strict rules and regulations within whatever system you believe. When I was a kid in high school, I never understood why there is a Democratic Party, and a Republican Party, and an Independent Party. I thought the desire was to be "we the people." But we have these different party systems that have their own dogma, their own rules and regulations. But, not good or bad, I feel we have these because it's easier for us to just say, "OK, these are the rules that I'm going to live by because I'm a so-and-so; therefore, I'm just going to check out. When difficult things come at me, they will be measured by these ten beliefs that I have within this religion or political party." That's when I think we get into fights because we don't allow grey. We don't allow that question that came out of nowhere that we can't fit into our belief box or can't answer through one of these rules and regulations that we set up for ourselves to be scrutinized. It's just a lot easier to go through life identifying ourselves as a this or a that, and not really thinking about the substance of whatever issue or whatever challenge is confronting us. I understand that it feels icky sometimes to operate in the grey because we can feel like we're not centered. But, it's actually that centeredness that allows us to live in that grey.

Centeredness is only possible if it's built on a solid foundation. You can't build a penthouse on a foundation that's made of quicksand. From an organizational stand-point, you have to have certain foundational things in place in order for you to layer more complex issues on top of it. I'd imagine there's some kind of foundation you need to build with each horse too.

Dustin:
Absolutely.

Paul:
Additionally, if you've built a personal life foundation that's really solid, then you can pile on anything that comes at you, and it won't break. You won't break. You'll be able to live through that, lead through that. But, if you don't have that foundation, then it doesn't matter what comes at you. It could be something really tiny that just completely blows you over.

That's why I think it's important to keep coming back to these simple themes. However, a lot of people find this approach to be slow-moving and pedantic, but I'm a big believer in going slow to go fast.

Dustin:
That's smart.

Paul:

So many people want to get to the shiny object, to get to that exciting thing. But, if you haven't built a solid foundation, then you'll eventually have nothing. You built on quicksand.

Dustin:

It's very much that way with horses. I lay a solid foundation in the colts and I love it. I mean, I live for starting these horses. And, you know, getting them going in life. If you think about their progress on a scale from one to ten, everybody wants to get to box ten right away. That's the most important box to them. But the thing I've found, is everything starts and is built upon in box zero. If you skip box zero, and you try and start at one, when you get to ten, the foundation you need is not there.

Paul:

Exactly.

Dustin:

And I've had a bunch of horses come in here that are at box five, or six, or seven, and they skipped zero. I go back and I restart those horses at zero, and their owners complain, "What are you doing? They are here in box seven!" And I say, "Because he doesn't have this, and this should have been taught to him right off the bat. And, I'm gonna cure his current problems when I fix this part in box zero." I mean, you think about it, we build a foundation so strong under our homes that it can withhold earthquakes and everything else. I mean, you see some of these earthquakes that completely level houses, but their foundations are still there. They might be cracked but the foundation is still there. You can rebuild. So, why don't we build those foundations into our horses, ourselves, our organizations?

Paul:
GREY LEADERSHIP® requires that foundation which allows us to operate successfully in the grey. That horse can then make creative decisions later as long as that foundation is there.

Dustin:
Yep.

Paul:
People don't like box zero. Box zero is just that, empty, but it's got to be filled first in order to operate in the grey that lies ahead.

Dustin:
I live in a grey world. What can I say?

You taught me something about myself, Paul. I always have end games. I have goals. I know where I want to be and where I want to go. However, I also have morals and ethics that I live by. Things I will and things I won't do.

Paul:
That's the structure we talked about within the grey.

But this, ⟿ my friend, is grey.

Dustin:
Exactly. That's me in real life. I'm gonna frame that and put it on my wall.

Paul:
We're going to put that in the book.

Dustin:
I like it. "How Dustin actually lives his life."

Paul:
Dustin, before the book:

Dustin, after the book:

Dustin:
There you go. I love it.

Connecting the Dots

As a baby, we naturally fell back on our instincts of survival. Do we have enough food, water, and even sleep? We were focused on what *we* needed, not what the rest of our family needed at that moment. If that is how we came into this world, spending our early years focused solely on ourselves, it is only reasonable to understand why that inclination might stay with us throughout our entire life.

So then, as leaders, as friends, and as family, we cannot forget this primal question that sits in the background of everything we experience, "What's in it for me?" Additionally, we have to keep in mind that this question, at its essence, does not focus on what is mutually best for us and the company or the relationship. It is literally asking, "What real benefit, if any, do *I* get out of this decision, out of this change?" The fact that perhaps everyone in the company will get raises, have more time for strategic thinking, and upgrade the office experience is superfluous if that change also involves moving to another cubicle, or dare we say another building altogether. Big changes like that can be enough for you to not be on board with the change simply because you had to make a change that you did not want. You had to move to that new cubicle. A recent example of this occurred at a major gaming company in Los Angeles. The human resource specialist told us that the company was having difficulty after a merger with another company because the new office location did not allow for many of the workers to eat at their favorite lunch place. This was disrupting the workplace and taking up valuable time and energy to address. Absolutely tragic.

In order to avoid this kind of impediment, it is vital to be proactive and fully understand each and every person you work with or with whom you have a relationship. You need to know their basic drivers. Then you must match those with the kind of change you are putting into place so that you answer that important question of *what's in it for me* before they even ask it.

Chances are you will not be able to make every single person happy as each has their own unique needs and desires. This is where the ability to operate in the grey is critical. While we need some structure to analyze the situation and make decisions, we also need to stay flexible within it to be able to deliver creative solutions that cut down the middle, as Dustin states, to sincerely please the majority of the people affected. This grey technique also assists in dealing with all the obstacles that will pop up along the way. If you train yourself to be extremely adaptable within a structured framework, you will have the most success with managing change, no matter how many are in your human herd.

Cowboy-Conductor Challenge

While it might seem counter to what you think of leadership, getting to intimately know each and every person under your care is a valuable tool. It is not enough to know your employee's birthday, or their kids' names, or when they started in the company.

Find out what your employees aspire to, what their passions are, and what they love to do in their spare time. This will help you understand what drives their decisions, their actions, and their end goals. Yes, it takes time. But the time spent in understanding them will pale in comparison to the time spent countering their unhappiness when change is introduced to them.

Identify what your non-negotiables are, those things that, despite your compassion for their situation, are non-starters. This provides the structure within the grey you will need to operate. Then, identify all of the grey items you are willing to allow as you move through the change with them.

Use the power of empathy to connect to those who show resistance. There are many reasons why people resist. It could be a personal or family situation that is unknown, their career history and goals, the degree the change will affect them personally, the success or failure of past changes in the organization, the organization's culture, or the change saturation rate in the recent past. All of these play into the decision to accept or resist change and our human tendency to repel it.

As we discussed at the end of this conversation, life's trajectory is not a straight arrow; it is a squirrely one. Understand that. Prepare for it. Plan for it. If you can operate within the grey, within the unknown, you will not be thrown by any arrow that life shoots at you personally or professionally.

Saddle up. Identify the themes. Ride it out. Conduct yourself in a manner that benefits all of those in your care.

ROUNDIN' 'EM UP

Throughout this book, we have holistically explored GREY LEADERSHIP®. The term seems counterintuitive. Grey? Leadership? At first glance, they do not go together as well as, perhaps, RED LEADERSHIP because we all prefer definitive terms, definitive views. Yet we both have found that, throughout our lives, we have been the most successful and the most satisfied when operating in the grey. It has allowed us to *freely move our feet* as well as convincingly move the feet of others. It has allowed us to be authentically present with ourselves and with others.

Paul:

Speaking of moving other peoples' feet, I remember the moment I knew I had harnessed GREY LEADERSHIP®. I was on the stage of Orchestra Hall in Minneapolis conducting a concert of the top, pre-collegiate orchestra of the Greater Twin Cities Youth Symphonies. We were about to perform the *Nimrod* movement from Edward Elgar's *Enigma Variations* when the grey finally came into focus for me.

It had been over a month of rehearsing this particular movement without success. To perform this delicate yet powerful piece requires patience, purpose, and passion. It begins with the most quiet notes in the strings, barely audible. Then, for over four minutes and thirty seconds it continues to turn up the volume moment by moment, note by note, instrument by instrument, building to the fullest and loudest climax with the entire orchestra engaged before it retreats back into absolute silence over a meticulously paced twenty seconds.

As you can imagine, it is challenging to focus pre-college musicians, no matter how brilliantly talented they are, to perform such a feat with the sustainable intensity this piece requires to move an audience to tears. While we had our moments in the rehearsals leading up to this performance, it never, ever fully worked as the emotional architecture of sound it was written to be.

During that same concert, we were honoring a much beloved conductor who had been with the organization for decades and with whom the majority of the orchestra had known and played for during a great deal of their childhood. As I gave my introductory remarks to the audience just before we performed *Nimrod*, I looked around the stage and noticed the energy coming off of each and every one of those musicians and realized, in that moment, what they needed. It was then that I sincerely, albeit spontaneously, dedicated the performance of *Nimrod* to James Berg, their long-time mentor and musical friend.

I'll never forget the palpable focus I felt when I turned back around to face the orchestra. They had heard the dedication to Maestro Berg and were ready to respond. I picked up my baton, closed my eyes, and gave the motion to begin. What happened over the next glorious four minutes and thirty seconds profoundly changed my life. I encouraged them through my *authentic presence* to fully give themselves up to the music, with the driving philosophy of allowing them to *move their feet* while addressing their question of *what's in it for me* before they even knew they were asking it.

To this day, a conducting colleague who attended the performance tells me, "It remains the musical highlight of my life, one of the most beautiful things I've ever heard."

That was the *power of empowerment.*

Dustin:

Many like to call me a horse whisperer. As if I wave some illusive magic wand that other people fail to grasp. It's not that at all. I have given in to the grey as many of my mentors before me have and found a space to operate harmoniously with the horse.

For me, GREY LEADERSHIP® was not a singular defining moment, but instead, a lifetime of experiences and lessons learned from the horse that guided me to this style of horsemanship. It's beyond just handling them. It's digging deeper and looking at the holistic needs of the animal and setting the human emotions and ego aside, purely letting go and succumbing to what the horse presents and responding in a way it understands.

I talk about it all the time that I wish I could go back to some of the first horses I worked with and be able to rub them and give them a better deal with the tools I have today. This style of horsemanship is truly a journey with no destination, but instead a process of leaving the shallow end and swimming towards the deep end of the pond of life.

It's exercising relationship-building on their terms and leaving the black and white behind and delving into the grey. Let's be clear, I still have boundaries and expectations of the horse that are black and white. Such as, I will not let a horse push on me. I am the lead horse, but I travel through the grey with each horse to establish that boundary.

A good example of the grey is to achieve straightness in a horse. It requires thousands and thousands of bends. It's not a matter of putting on rose-colored glasses and accepting what you get. It's elevating your thinking to get to your ultimate destination or goal.

GREY LEADERSHIP® will not only vastly improve your relationship with the horse, but if you truly embrace it, it will change your life for the better. Guided through empathy and compassion, it removes the human tendency to be judgmental and negative and opens the door to a healthier, happy life of fulfilling relationships.

Couldn't we all use a little more of that in our life?

Remember, GREY LEADERSHIP® is the boundless, non-binary approach to complex issues using a foundational framework yielding transformational results.

While the end goal, the final result or impact is important, the journey you take and the tools you use to get there are ultimately more critical. They signal who you are, what drives you and how you view others and the world around you.

The essentials of GREY LEADERSHIP® are:

⇒ Finding the trifecta of life: the skills that rank you at the top tenth percentile amongst your peers around the globe, the one thing that you are the most passionate about, and the vocation that combines skills and passion while compensating you on your fulfilling life journey

⇒ Making others your number one priority, your absolute focus, driving how you approach them and how you develop your relationship with them

⇒ Believing that anything is possible and never letting failure stop you from achieving your dreams or keeping you from discovering your *aha-moment*

⇒ Identifying, embracing, and acting on those internal foundational attributes that we all share as human beings

⇒ Showing up as the best person you can be to gain the respect and, more importantly, the trust of others, allowing you to engage in healthy conflict, buoy accountability, and eliminate micromanagement

⇒ Unleashing the power that is already in those you lead by creating an owner-operated environment where they have both the responsibility *and* the authority to accomplish greatness

⇒ Celebrating the qualities of those around you by tapping into each person's awareness, personality, posture, and presence while maintaining your sense of curiosity, humility, and centeredness

⇒ Opening up the world of possibility by boosting your potential and tapping into your Three Cs: Curiosity, Creativity, and Commitment

⇒ Adopting a *nothing is as it seems* approach to the world around you and allowing multi-angled questioning to be an insightful strategy for verification by not giving into the Assumption Xceleration Theory™

⇒ Being aware of *being aware* and constantly monitoring your internal motivation as well as your authentic connectivity to others

⇒ Looking beyond the obvious by fueling your curiosity, leading you to a creative and imaginative approach to connecting the dots

⇒ Gaining a deeper meaning of the universe by being present in your words and actions with the intent to understand, not to respond

⇒ Choosing your words and tone to signal your intent and affect greater impact

⇒ Proactively and fully understanding everyone's basic life-drivers to be able to answer the question of *what's in it for me* before they ask it in order for you to lead change more efficiently, effectively, and exponentially

As we discussed at the beginning of this book, GREY LEADERSHIP® requires the awareness of what it means, the desire to cultivate it, the knowledge of how to attain it, and the ability to use it correctly.

Whether you are a cowboy, conductor, CEO, team leader, staff member, volunteer, friend, parent, sibling, or spouse, GREY LEADERSHIP® is for you.

GREY LEADERSHIP® is an art and must be practiced regularly to achieve its full benefits. Allow yourself the time it takes to build upon your daily accomplishments. GREY LEADERSHIP® requires you to completely let go while at the same time commanding an intentional discipline and structure within which to operate. It seems contradictory. But allowing these two apparently opposing forces to live within the same galaxy of possibility is what will make you, as a grey leader, dramatically out-perform your peers.

Possessing GREY LEADERSHIP® will give you the freedom to experience the joy of knowing that everything you do and everything you say will have a profound transformational effect on everyone within your orbit, allowing you to achieve wildly high levels of success both personally and professionally. How grey-t would that be?!

Take your first step and Be the GREY™!

ACKNOWLEDGMENTS

We would like to thank all who helped us with this book, from those who allowed us the time and space to gather our thoughts to those who helped make it so much better with their editing assistance.

First and foremost, our deepest love and appreciation to our wives Aimee Davis and Cynthia Lewis who supported us every minute during the writing, editing, and launching of this book.

We also thank our prereaders who helped us hone in on the important parts that make the reader's experience even more personal: Charlotte Davis, Robert Eckert, Carole Hines, John Holliday, Mathew Knowles, Kathy Kolarik, Rochelle Lewis, David Lockington, Alan Mason, Nicholas McGegan, Jan Neuharth, and Chris Soltis.

Finally, we would like to acknowledge the countless people, and herds of horses, who have come into our lives and shaped us into who we are today both personally and professionally. For you, we are forever grateful.

ABOUT THE AUTHORS

Dustin Davis

Dustin Davis is an A-
merican cowboy, in-
structor, clinician, and
co-author of his debut
book *Cowboys & Con-
ductors: Conversations
in Horsemanship-Hu-
manship.* Dustin was
born and raised in Col-
orado and now calls Southern California home with his
wife Aimee, daughter Hensley, and a hundred plus horses,
cattle, and dogs.

Dustin currently operates a horsemanship barn and
also travels the country offering horsemanship clinics
helping horses and their humans. Dustin grew up as a 4H
kid training and winning many top honors with his
market hogs and showmanship. Through 4H, Dustin also
gained a strong aptitude and keen eye for animal judging
culminating with a collegiate scholarship opportunity for
judging. Upon graduating high school he ran a 38,000-
acre cattle ranch where he took care of the livestock,
handled the daily tasks, and took care of the ranch for the
corporation that owned it. He is a third-generation

auctioneer and followed in his father's and grandfather's footsteps attending auctioneering college and selling everything from horses to cars. Dustin also operated a horse transport business that led to him to exporting and transporting thousands of horses, from miniature horses, to the first mammoth mule to go overseas, to the International Federation for Equestrian Sports World Equestrian Games Gold Medal winning Reining team, to the Big 12 conference collegiate equestrian teams, and many more.

Dustin is a cowboy and embodies all that it entails including a lifestyle where horses and livestock come first. He is a student of the founders of Natural Horsemanship, Ray Hunt and Tom Dorrance, and their successors. Dustin has a true gift of understanding how horses think and communicate and he utilizes that to work with them and their owners to build a confidant relationship and deep bond.

Dustin's training methods, known as GREY LEADER-SHIP®, exemplify a servant-leadership style versus a traditional-leadership style in that the power is shared with the horse and that the needs of the horse come first which helps it develop and perform as highly as possible. Ray Hunt always says, "I haven't found a horse these methods don't work for," and Dustin agrees with this philosophy and is carrying on the legacy of these great horsemen. There is a very logical and fundamental connection between these methods and *humanship* as discussed in the book and how the methods Dustin uses for horses can be used for humans and business relationships alike.

Paul Jan Zdunek

After a decade-long career as an orchestra conductor, Paul Jan Zdunek brings over 20 years of C-Suite experience providing business leadership and advisory services for middle market companies, family businesses, and charitable organizations. He has been a business transformation advis-

or, change management leader, and interim executive for institutions requiring financial or organizational revitalization. Paul is often engaged by organizations wanting to reimagine the foundational strategies of purpose, people, and place, focusing on market differentiation, human capital resources, and organizational development and culture.

Paul's expertise includes organizational and leadership development, change management, conflict and crisis resolution, complex facilitation, personal and professional coaching, philanthropic strategy, as well as stakeholder management.

Paul is a PROSCI® Certified Change Management Professional and Certified Exit Planning Advisor, CEPA®. He has taught at the University of Southern California's Sol Price School of Public Policy, as well as within the graduate Arts Administration program at Goucher College in Maryland, and continues to deliver keynote speeches at industry conferences and executive retreats, including Vistage Worldwide, on the topics of organizational transformation and sustainable success. He serves on the

Board of Directors for a number of private and charitable organizations and is the co-author of a book on cultivating GREY LEADERSHIP® titled *Cowboys & Conductors: Conversations on Horseman-Humanship.*

Paul has a Bachelor of Music in Composition from The Johns Hopkins University Peabody Institute, a Master of Music in Orchestral Conducting from The Cleveland Institute of Music, and an MBA from the Peter F. Drucker School of Management at Claremont Graduate University.

ABOUT ATMOSPHERE PRESS

Atmosphere Press is an independent, full-service publisher for excellent books in all genres and for all audiences. Learn more about what we do at atmospherepress.com.

We encourage you to check out some of Atmosphere's latest releases, which are available at Amazon.com and via order from your local bookstore:

The Swing: A Muse's Memoir About Keeping the Artist Alive, by Susan Dennis
Possibilities with Parkinson's: A Fresh Look, by Dr. C
Gaining Altitude - Retirement and Beyond, by Rebecca Milliken
Out and Back: Essays on a Family in Motion, by Elizabeth Templeman
Just Be Honest, by Cindy Yates
You Crazy Vegan: Coming Out as a Vegan Intuitive, by Jessica Ang
Detour: Lose Your Way, Find Your Path, by S. Mariah Rose
To B&B or Not to B&B: Deromanticizing the Dream, by Sue Marko
Convergence: The Interconnection of Extraordinary Experiences, by Barbara Mango and Lynn Miller
Sacred Fool, by Nathan Dean Talamantez
My Place in the Spiral, by Rebecca Beardsall
My Eight Dads, by Mark Kirby
Dinner's Ready! Recipes for Working Moms, by Rebecca Cailor